Pope Francis's words once again refresh the spirit! He follows his namesake, the saint from Assisi, in celebrating what God has created, our humanity. In these selected passages Pope Francis holds up our families as those intimate relationships through which we truly learn to love as we have been loved.

—Wendy M. Wright, Ph.D., author, *Sacred Dwelling* and *Seasons of a Family's Life*

This collection of Pope Francis's reflections, insights, practical guidance, and humorous comments on marriage and the family provides further confirmation, if any were needed, that he is a true pastor who knows the full spectrum of family life with its joys and sorrows, hopes and dreams. It makes available to a wide audience his positive approach to this whole subject. Alicia von Stamwitz is to be complimented for putting the pieces together in this highly readable and inspiring book.

—Gerard O'Connell, associate editor and Vatican correspondent for *America* magazine

Pope Francis has crafted homilies, formal writings and even Twitter messages to offer the faithful plentiful wisdom on living and loving within the context of our daily family life. In *The Blessing of Family*, noted author Alicia von Stamwitz cultivates our Holy Father's accessible wisdom into a format that is a helpful tool for today's family. Perfect to read around the dinner table or as part of your daily family prayer, this book belongs in every Catholic home!

—Lisa M. Hendey, author, *The Grace of Yes*
and founder of CatholicMom.com

THE
Blessing
OF
Family

~~~

INSPIRING WORDS
FROM
Pope
Francis

~~~

POPE FRANCIS
EDITED BY ALICIA VON STAMWITZ

Franciscan
MEDIA
Cincinnati, Ohio

The Blessing of Family is published in collaboration with the Libreria
Editrice Vaticana. All excerpts © 2015, Libreria Editrice Vaticana
and used by permission.

Cover and book design by Mark Sullivan
Cover image © Giampiero Sposito | Reuters

LIBRARY OF CONGRESS CATALOGING-IN-PUBLICATION DATA

Francis, Pope, 1936-
[Works. Selections. English]
The blessing of family : inspiring words from Pope Francis / Pope Francis
; edited by Alicia von Stamwitz.
pages cm
ISBN 978-1-61636-909-5 (acid-free paper)
1. Families—Religious aspects—Catholic Church. I. Stamwitz, Alicia
von. II. Catholic Church. Pope (2013- : Francis) III. Title.
BX2351.F7313 2015
261.8'3585—dc23
                    2015008013

ISBN 978-1-61636-909-5

Published by Franciscan Media
28 W. Liberty St.
Cincinnati, OH 45202
www.FranciscanMedia.org
www.AmericanCatholic.org

Printed in the United States of America.
Printed on acid-free paper.
15 16 17 18 19 5 4 3 2 1

Contents

Introduction

Pope Francis cares deeply about the health and happiness today's families. Just seven months into his papacy, he announced that he would host an Extraordinary General Assembly of the Synod of Bishops to discuss the pastoral challenges facing modern families. Only twice before in the fifty years since Pope Paul VI established the Synod of Bishops has a pope called an "extraordinary" synod, which signals the urgency and importance of the chosen theme. The discussions on the family began in October 2013 in Rome, and they have since sparked conversations in millions of homes and parishes around the world.

The pope continues to keep the theme of the family in the forefront through his speeches, homilies, addresses, and writings, and he is quick to share anecdotes from his childhood in Argentina to illustrate his points. Jorge was the eldest of the five children born to Mario and Regina Bergoglio, first-generation Italian immigrants. He grew up in a middle-class family in Buenos Aires near the home of his paternal grandmother Rosa, whose enchanting lessons in faith sparked youthful devotion. But Jorge was not an overly pious boy: he played soccer and basketball, had a lively sense of humor, and liked to dance (the milonga more than the tango, for those who care to know). Although he was a voracious reader and a strong student, he preferred the outdoors to any indoor activity, including listening to the radio or practicing piano. When his mother became seriously ill after giving birth to his youngest sister, Jorge learned to cook for the family and discovered that he enjoyed cooking—especially pasta and "a good meat stew." As a teenager, he worked as a janitor at the stocking factory where his father worked as an accountant. Before joining the Jesuits, a religious order of priests, he studied chemistry and worked for a few years as a technologist in the foods section of a local laboratory. He doubted his vocation once, early in his seminary days, after meeting a certain girl at a family wedding. Her beauty and intellectual radiance "dazzled" him and left him sleepless for a week.

Pope Francis's rich and varied life experience helps explain his knack for painting a colorful picture of family life or giving a memorable lesson on love and forgiveness. "I always give this advice to newlyweds," he says: "Argue as much as you like. If the plates fly, let them! But never end the day without making peace! Never!"

In this book, Pope Francis addresses the splendor and struggles of married love, the joys and troubles of ordinary Christian families, and the family's mission to be leaven in the world. He speaks from the heart more often than not, almost as if he were seated beside you at a kitchen table. That is intentional on his part: he prefers simple words to prepared speeches because he genuinely wants to connect with each person he encounters. As you begin this book, try to imagine Pope Francis sitting with you and conversing with you, as a good friend or family member might do, his eyes bright with warmth and his voice brimming with encouragement.

Whether you are young or old, married or single, engaged, widowed, or divorced, may Pope Francis's words strengthen you, refresh you, and illuminate the pages of your own life story.

—*Alicia von Stamwitz,*
editor

CHAPTER ONE

~ The Splendor of Love and Marriage ~

We are created in order to love, as a reflection of God and his love…. When a man and woman celebrate the Sacrament of Matrimony, God as it were "is mirrored" in them; he impresses in them his own features and the indelible character of his love. Marriage is the icon of God's love for us.

—POPE FRANCIS, APRIL 2, 2014

THE IMAGE OF GOD IS LOVE

At the beginning of the Book of Genesis, the first book of the Bible, at the culmination of the creation account it says: "God created man in his own image, in the image of God he created him; male and female he created them.... Therefore a man leaves his father and his mother and cleaves to his wife, and they become one flesh" (Gen 1:27; 2:24). The image of God is the married couple: the man and the woman; not only the man, not only the woman, but both of them together. This is the image of God: love. God's covenant with us is represented in that covenant between man and woman. And this is very beautiful!

GENERAL AUDIENCE, ST. PETER'S SQUARE
WEDNESDAY, APRIL 2, 2014

THE CALL OF THE LORD

What is marriage? It is a true and authentic vocation, as are the priesthood and religious life. Two Christians who marry have recognized the call of the Lord in their own love story, the vocation to form one flesh and one life from two, male and female. And the Sacrament of Holy Matrimony envelops this love in the grace of God, it roots it in God himself. By this gift, and by the certainty of this call, you can continue on assured; you have nothing to fear; you can face everything together!

ADDRESS TO THE YOUNG PEOPLE OF UMBRIA, BASILICA
OF ST. MARY OF THE ANGELS SQUARE, ASSISI
FRIDAY, OCTOBER 4, 2013

HAND IN HAND

Those who celebrate the Sacrament of Marriage say, "I promise to be true to you, in joy and in sadness, in sickness and in health; I will love you and honor you all the days of my life." At that moment, the couple does not know what will happen, nor what joys and pains await them. They are setting out, like Abraham, on a journey together. And that is what marriage is! Setting out and walking together, hand in hand, putting yourselves in the Lord's powerful hands. Hand in hand, always and for the rest of your lives.

ADDRESS TO PARTICIPANTS IN THE PILGRIMAGE OF
FAMILIES, ST. PETER'S SQUARE
SATURDAY, OCTOBER 26, 2013

Pope Francis @Pontifex · February 14, 2014
"Dear young people, don't be afraid to marry. A faithful and fruitful marriage will bring you happiness."

THE ROCK OF TRUE LOVE

What do we mean by "love"? Is it only a feeling, a psychophysical state? Certainly, if that is it, then we cannot build on anything solid. But if instead love is a relationship, then it is a reality that grows, and we can also say by way of example that it is built up like a home. And a home is built together, not alone! To build something here means to foster and aid growth. Dear engaged couples, you are preparing to grow together, to build this home, to live together forever. You do not want to found it on the sand of sentiments, which come and go, but on the rock of true love, the love that comes from God. The family is born from this plan of love, it wants to grow just as a home is built, as a place of affection, of help, of hope, of support…. Living together is an art—a patient, beautiful, fascinating journey. It does not end once you have won each other's love…. Rather, it is precisely there where it begins!

ADDRESS TO ENGAGED COUPLES PREPARING FOR
MARRIAGE, ST. PETER'S SQUARE
FRIDAY, FEBRUARY 14, 2014

A Total Gift of Self

In marriage we give ourselves completely, without calculation or reserve, sharing everything—gifts and hardships—and trusting in God's Providence. This is the experience that the young can learn from their parents and grandparents. It is an experience of faith in God and of mutual trust, profound freedom, and holiness—because holiness presumes giving oneself with fidelity and sacrifice every day of one's life! But there are problems in marriage. There are always different points of view, jealousy, arguing. We need to say to young spouses that they should never end the day without making peace. The Sacrament of Marriage is renewed in this act of peace after an argument, a misunderstanding, a hidden jealousy, even a sin. Making peace gives unity to the family. Tell young people, young couples, that it is not easy to go down this path, but it is a very beautiful path, very beautiful.

ADDRESS TO MEMBERS OF THE PONTIFICAL COUNCIL
FOR THE FAMILY, CLEMENTINE HALL
FRIDAY, OCTOBER 25, 2013

The Power of a Changed Heart

Love is the greatest power for the transformation of reality because it pulls down the walls of selfishness and fills the ditches that keep us apart. This is the love that comes from a changed heart, from a heart of stone that has been turned into a heart of flesh, a human heart. And this is what grace does, the grace of Jesus Christ which we have all received.

ADDRESS TO CONVENTION OF THE DIOCESE OF ROME
PAUL VI AUDIENCE HALL
MONDAY, JUNE 17, 2013

Pope Francis @Pontifex · October 8, 2013

"The secret of Christian living is love. Only love fills the empty spaces caused by evil."

Revolutionary Love

Today, there are those who say that marriage is out of fashion. Is it out of fashion? In a culture of relativism and the ephemeral, many preach the importance of "enjoying" the moment. They say that it is not worth making a life-long commitment, making a definitive decision, "for ever," because we do not know what tomorrow will bring. I ask you, instead, to be revolutionaries. I ask you to swim against the tide. Yes, I am asking you to rebel against this culture that sees everything as temporary and that ultimately believes you are incapable of responsibility, that believes you are incapable of true love. I have confidence in you and I pray for you. Have the courage "to swim against the tide." And also have the courage to be happy.

ADDRESS TO THE XXVIII WORLD YOUTH DAY
VOLUNTEERS, RIO DE JANEIRO
SUNDAY, JULY 28, 2013

A Gift to Be Cultivated

The Church's concern for the family begins with the proper preparation and appropriate support of spouses, as well as the faithful and clear explanation of the Church's doctrine on marriage and on the family. Sacramental marriage is a gift of God as well as a commitment. The love of two spouses is sanctified by Christ, and a married couple is called to bear witness to and cultivate this sanctity through their faithful love for one another.

ADDRESS TO THE BISHOPS OF AUSTRIA, "AD LIMINA" VISIT
THURSDAY, JANUARY 30, 2014

Pope Francis @Pontifex · May 9, 2014

"Holiness means giving ourselves in sacrifice every day. And so married life is a tremendous path to sanctity!"

Steadfast in Fidelity

God surprises us with his love, but he demands that we be faithful in following him. We can be unfaithful, but he cannot: he is "the faithful one," and he demands of us that same fidelity. Think of all the times when we were excited about something or other, some initiative, some task, but afterwards, at the first sign of difficulty, we threw in the towel. Sadly, this also happens in the case of fundamental decisions, such as marriage. It is the difficulty of remaining steadfast, faithful to decisions we have made and to commitments we have made. Often it is easy enough to say "yes," but then we fail to repeat this "yes" each and every day. We fail to be faithful.

HOMILY, ST. PETER'S SQUARE
SUNDAY, OCTOBER 13, 2013

THREE ESSENTIAL WORDS

Sometimes we do things which are not good and which harm others. It is important to have the courage to ask for forgiveness when we are at fault in the family. Some weeks ago, in this very square, I said that in order to have a healthy family, three words need to be used. And I want to repeat these three words: please, thank you, sorry. Three essential words! We say please so as not to be forceful in family life: "May I please do this? Would you be happy if I did this?" We do this with a language that seeks agreement. We say thank you, thank you for love!

Be honest with me, how many times do you say thank you to your wife, and you to your husband? How many days go by *without* uttering this word?

And the last word: sorry. We all make mistakes, and on occasion someone gets offended in the marriage, in the family…and harsh words are spoken. But please listen to my advice: don't ever let the sun set without reconciling. Peace is made each day in the family.

ADDRESS TO PARTICIPANTS IN THE PILGRIMAGE OF
FAMILIES, ST. PETER'S SQUARE
SATURDAY, OCTOBER 26, 2013

GOOD AND EVIL IN OUR HEARTS

What is in our heart: is it love? Let us think: do I love my parents, my children, my wife, my husband, people in the neighborhood, the sick? Do I love? Is there hate? Do I hate someone? Often we find hatred, don't we? "I love everyone except for this one, this one, and that one!" That's hatred, isn't it?

What is in my heart: is it forgiveness? Is there an attitude of forgiveness for those who have offended me? Or is there an attitude of revenge: "He will pay for it!"

We must ask ourselves what is within, because what is inside comes out and harms if it is evil. And if it is good, it comes out and does good. It is beautiful to tell ourselves the truth, and to feel ashamed when we are in a situation that is not what God wants.

HOMILY, SAN TOMMASO APOSTOLO PARISH
SUNDAY, FEBRUARY 16, 2014

TOUCHED BY MERCY

Jesus is the incarnation of the Living God, the one who brings life amid so many deeds of death, such as sin, selfishness and self-absorption. Jesus accepts, loves, uplifts, encourages, forgives, restores the ability to walk, and gives back life. Throughout the Gospels we see how Jesus by his words and actions brings the transforming life of God. This was the experience of the woman who anointed the feet of the Lord with ointment: she felt understood, loved, and she responded by a gesture of love. She let herself be touched by God's mercy, she obtained forgiveness, and she started a new life. God, the Living One, is merciful.

HOMILY, ST. PETER'S SQUARE
SUNDAY, JUNE 16, 2013

Pope Francis @Pontifex · Feb 20, 2014

"Lord Jesus, make us capable of loving as you love."

God Always Forgives Us

The Bible shows us the human drama in all its reality: good and evil, passion, sin and its consequences. Whenever we want to assert ourselves, when we become wrapped up in our own selfishness and put ourselves in the place of God, we end up spawning death. King David's adultery is one example of this. Selfishness leads to lies, as we attempt to deceive ourselves and those around us. But God cannot be deceived. We heard how the prophet says to David: "Why have you done evil in the Lord's sight?" (cf. 2 Sam 12:9). The king is forced to face his deeds of death. What he has done is truly a deed of death, not life! He recognizes what he has done and he begs forgiveness: "I have sinned against the Lord!" (v. 13). The God of mercy, who desires life and always forgives us, now forgives David and restores him to life. The prophet tells him: "The Lord has put away your sin; you shall not die."

HOMILY, ST. PETER'S SQUARE
SUNDAY, JUNE 16, 2013

LET JESUS ENTER YOUR LIFE

How often does Love have to ask us: "Why do you look for the living among the dead?" Our daily problems and worries can wrap us up in ourselves, in sadness and bitterness…and that is where death is. That is not the place to look for the One who is alive! Let the risen Jesus enter your life. Welcome him as a friend, with trust: he is life! If up till now you have kept him at a distance, step forward. He will receive you with open arms. If you have been indifferent, take a risk: you won't be disappointed. If following him seems difficult, don't be afraid. Trust him, be confident that he is close to you. He is with you, and he will give you the peace you are looking for and the strength to live as he would have you do.

HOMILY, VATICAN BASILICA
HOLY SATURDAY, MARCH 30, 2013

Pope Francis @Pontifex · January 17, 2015

"The com-passion of God, his suffering-with-us, gives meaning and worth to our struggles and our sufferings."

TRUST IN GOD'S FAITHFULNESS

With trust in God's faithfulness, everything can be faced responsibly and without fear. Christian spouses are not naïve; they know life's problems and temptations. But they are not afraid to be responsible before God and before society. They do not run away, they do not hide, they do not shirk the mission of forming a family and bringing children into the world.

You say to me, "But today, Father, it is difficult...."Of course it is difficult! That is why we need the grace, the grace that comes from the sacrament! The sacraments are not decorations in life: "What a beautiful marriage! What a beautiful ceremony! What a beautiful banquet!"...that is not the sacrament of marriage. That is a decoration!

Grace is not given to decorate life but rather to make us strong in life, giving us courage to go forward! And without isolating oneself but always staying together. Christians celebrate the Sacrament of Marriage because they know they need it! They need it to stay together and to carry out their mission as parents. "In joy and in sadness, in sickness and in health."

ADDRESS TO PARTICIPANTS IN THE PILGRIMAGE
OF FAMILIES, ST. PETER'S SQUARE
SATURDAY, OCTOBER 26, 2013

PILLARS OF STRENGTH

Let us think about our parents, about our grandparents and great grandparents: they married in much poorer conditions than our own. Some married during wartime or just after a war. Some like my own parents emigrated. Where did they find the strength? They found it in the certainty that the Lord was with them, that their families were blessed by God through the Sacrament of Matrimony, and that the mission of bringing children into the world and educating them is also blessed. With this assurance they overcame even the most difficult trials. These were simple certainties, but they were real; they were the pillars that supported their love. Their lives were not easy; there were problems, many, many problems. However, these simple assurances helped them to go forward. And they succeeded in having beautiful families, and in giving life and in raising their children.

ADDRESS TO THE YOUNG PEOPLE OF UMBRIA, BASILICA
OF ST. MARY OF THE ANGELS SQUARE, ASSISI
FRIDAY, OCTOBER 4, 2013

A True Bond

We are well aware of how many difficulties two spouses experience…. The important thing is to keep alive their bond with God, who stands as the foundation of the marital bond. And the true bond is always the Lord. When the family prays, the bond is preserved. When the husband prays for his wife and the wife prays for her husband, that bond becomes strong; one praying for the other.

GENERAL AUDIENCE, ST. PETER'S SQUARE
WEDNESDAY, APRIL 2, 2014

Pope Francis @Pontifex · Oct 1, 2013

"Do we truly pray? Without an abiding relationship with God, it is difficult to live an authentic and consistent Christian life."

AFTER THE PLATES FLY, MAKE PEACE!

It is normal for a husband and wife to quarrel…. Perhaps you were mad, perhaps plates flew, but please remember this: never let the sun go down without making peace! Never, never, never! This is a secret, a secret for maintaining love and making peace. Pretty words are not necessary. Sometimes just a simple gesture and peace is made….

If you let the day end without making peace, the next day, what is inside of you is cold and hardened, and it is even more difficult to make peace. Remember: never let the sun go down without making peace!

ADDRESS TO ENGAGED COUPLES PREPARING FOR
MARRIAGE, ST. PETER'S SQUARE
FRIDAY, FEBRUARY 14, 2014

Sanctified by Christ's Love

The love of Christ, which has blessed and sanctified the union of husband and wife, is able to sustain their love and to renew it when, humanly speaking, it becomes lost, wounded or worn out. The love of Christ can restore to spouses the joy of journeying together. This is what marriage is all about: man and woman walking together, wherein the husband helps his wife to become ever more a woman, and wherein the woman has the task of helping her husband to become ever more a man. This is the task that you both share.

"I love you, and for this love I help you to become ever more a woman."

"I love you, and for this love I help you to become ever more a man."

Here we see the reciprocity of differences. The path is not always a smooth one, free of disagreements: otherwise it would not be human. It is a demanding journey, at times difficult, and at times turbulent, but such is life!

HOMILY, ST. PETER'S SQUARE
SUNDAY, SEPTEMBER 14, 2014

A GESTURE CAN RESTORE PEACE

It is true that there are so many difficulties in married life, so many, when there is insufficient work or money, when the children have problems…and many times the husband and wife become a little fractious and argue between themselves….Yet we must not become saddened by this. Love is stronger than the moment when there is arguing, and therefore I always advise spouses: do not let a day when you have argued end without making peace. Always! And to make peace it isn't necessary to call the United Nations to come to the house and make peace. A little gesture is sufficient, a caress, and then let it be!

GENERAL AUDIENCE, ST. PETER'S SQUARE
WEDNESDAY, APRIL 2, 2014

Pope Francis @Pontifex · Dec 16, 2014

"It is so important to listen! Husbands and wives need to communicate to bring happiness and serenity to family life."

Love Is Your Daily Bread

A marriage is not successful just because it endures; quality is important. To stay together and to know how to love one another forever is the challenge for Christian couples. What comes to mind is the miracle of the multiplication of the loaves: for you too, the Lord can multiply your love and give it to you fresh and good each day. He has an infinite reserve! He gives you the love that stands at the foundation of your union, and each day he renews and strengthens it. And he makes it ever greater when the family grows with children. On this journey prayer is important, it is necessary, always: he for her, she for him and both together. Ask Jesus to multiply your love. In the prayer of the Our Father we say: "Give us this day our daily bread." Spouses can also learn to pray like this: "Lord, give us this day our daily love," for the daily love of spouses is bread, the true bread of the soul, what sustains them in going forward.

ADDRESS TO ENGAGED COUPLES PREPARING FOR
MARRIAGE, ST. PETER'S SQUARE
FRIDAY, FEBRUARY 14, 2014

There Will Be Crosses

Marriage is a symbol of life, real life: it is not "fiction"! It is the sacrament of the love of Christ and the Church, a love which finds its proof and guarantee in the Cross. My desire for you is that you have a good journey, a fruitful one, growing in love. I wish you happiness. There will be crosses! But the Lord is always there to help us move forward. May the Lord bless you!

HOMILY, ST. PETER'S SQUARE
SUNDAY, SEPTEMBER 14, 2014

Pope Francis @Pontifex · Sep 28, 2013
"Every marriage has difficult moments. But these experiences of the Cross can make the path of love even stronger."

The Beauty of This Union

We need to ask ourselves how we can better prepare young people for marriage, so that they might discover ever more deeply the beauty of this union that, well founded on love and responsibility, is capable of overcoming trials, difficulties and selfishness with mutual forgiveness, repairing what risks being broken and not falling into the trap of a throw-away mindset.

ADDRESS OF POPE FRANCIS TO THE BISHOPS OF POLAND,
"AD LIMINA" VISIT
FRIDAY, FEBRUARY 7, 2014

Pope Francis @Pontifex · Mar 8, 2014

"The challenge for Christian spouses: remaining together, knowing how to love one another always, and doing so in a way that their love grows."

A VITAL CELL OF SOCIETY AND THE CHURCH

Marriage preparation must, as far as it is possible, be thorough. There are many threats to the family, which is the vital cell of society and the Church; thus, the family "needs to be protected and defended, so that it may offer society the service expected of it, that of providing men and women capable of building a social fabric of peace and harmony" (*Africae Munus*, n. 42). Moreover, families need more than ever to be supported on their journey of faith. May they find perseverance and strength in prayer, attentive to Sacred Scripture and the Sacraments!

ADDRESS TO THE BISHOPS OF MADAGASCAR,
"AD LIMINA" VISIT
FRIDAY, MARCH 28, 2014

CHAPTER TWO

~ The Family in God's Embrace ~

In the family, everything that enables us to grow, to mature and to live is given to each of us. We cannot grow up by ourselves, we cannot journey on our own, in isolation; rather, we journey and grow in a community, in a family.

—POPE FRANCIS, OCTOBER 9, 2013

Leaven in the Dough of Society

For the Christian community, the family is far more than a "theme." It is life: it is the daily fabric of life and the journey of generations, together in love, passing on their faith and fundamental moral values. It is concrete solidarity, effort, patience; and also a plan, hope, the future. All this—which the Christian community lives out in the light of faith, hope and charity—should never be kept to oneself but must become, every day, the leaven in the dough of all society for the highest common good.

MESSAGE TO PARTICIPANTS IN THE 47TH SOCIAL WEEK
OF ITALIAN CATHOLICS, FROM THE VATICAN
WEDNESDAY, SEPTEMBER 11, 2013

Do Not Stop Dreaming!

I am very fond of dreams in families. For nine months every mother and father dreams about their baby. Am I right? They dream about what kind of child he or she will be....You can't have a family without dreams. Once a family loses the ability to dream, children do not grow, love does not grow, life shrivels up and dies. So I ask you each evening, when you make your examination of conscience, to also ask yourselves this question: Today did I dream about my children's future? Today did I dream about the love of my husband, my wife? Did I dream about my parents and grandparents who have gone before me? Dreaming is very important. Especially dreaming in families. Do not lose this ability to dream!

How many difficulties in married life are resolved when we leave room for dreaming; when we stop for a moment to think of our spouse and dream about the goodness present in everything around us. So it is very important to reclaim love by what we do each day. Do not ever stop being newlyweds!

ADDRESS TO FAMILIES, MALL OF ASIA ARENA, MANILA
FRIDAY, JANUARY 16, 2015

A MOTHER'S HEARTBEAT

The womb which hosts us is the first "school" of communication, a place of listening and physical contact where we begin to familiarize ourselves with the outside world within a protected environment, with the reassuring sound of the mother's heartbeat. This encounter between two persons, so intimately related while still distinct from each other, an encounter so full of promise, is our first experience of communication. It is an experience which we all share, since each of us was born of a mother.

MESSAGE FOR 49TH WORLD COMMUNICATIONS DAY,
FROM THE VATICAN
FRIDAY, JANUARY 23, 2015

THE SEAL OF UNCONDITIONAL LOVE

Children are loved before they arrive. How many times I find mothers in the square that want me to see their bellies and ask for my blessing! These children are loved before coming into the world. And this is free, this is love; they are loved before birth, like the love of God who loved us before birth. They are loved before having done anything to deserve it, before they can speak or think, even before coming into the world! Being children is the basic condition for knowing the love of God, which is the ultimate source of this real miracle. In the soul of every vulnerable child, God puts the seal of this love, which is the basis of human dignity, a dignity that nothing and no one can ever destroy.

GENERAL AUDIENCE, PAUL VI AUDIENCE HALL
WEDNESDAY, FEBRUARY 11, 2015

A CHILD CHANGES YOUR LIFE

Motherhood and fatherhood are a gift of God, but to accept the gift, to be astounded by its beauty and to make it shine in society, this is your task. Each of your children is a unique creature that will never be duplicated in the history of humanity. When one understands this, and that God wanted each one, we are astounded by how great a miracle a child is! A child changes your life!

ADDRESS TO THE NATIONAL NUMEROUS FAMILY
ASSOCIATION, PAUL VI AUDIENCE HALL
SUNDAY, DECEMBER 28, 2014

THANK GOD FOR NEWBORNS!

Today is the Feast of the Baptism of the Lord. This morning I baptized 32 infants. With you I thank the Lord for these creatures and for every new life. I am glad to baptize babies. I like it very much! Every newborn child is a gift of joy and hope, and each baby that is baptized is a miracle of faith and a celebration for the family of God.

ANGELUS, ST. PETER'S SQUARE
SUNDAY, JANUARY 12, 2014

Pope Francis @Pontifex · January 2, 2014

"God does not reveal himself in strength or power, but in the weakness and fragility of a newborn babe."

Signs of Hope and Social Health

The Child Jesus, born in Bethlehem, is the sign given by God to those who awaited salvation, and he remains forever the sign of God's tenderness and presence in our world. The angel announces to the shepherds: "This will be a sign for you: you will find a child...."

Today too, children are a sign. They are a sign of hope, a sign of life, but also a "diagnostic" sign, a marker indicating the health of families, society and the entire world. Wherever children are accepted, loved, cared for and protected, the family is healthy, society is more healthy and the world is more human.

HOMILY, MANGER SQUARE, BETHLEHEM
SUNDAY, MAY 25, 2014

CHILDREN ARE THE JOY OF SOCIETY

Children are the joy of the family and of society. They are not a question of reproductive biology, nor one of the many ways to fulfill oneself, much less a possession of their parents: No. Children are a gift, they are a gift. Understood? Children are a gift. Each one is unique and irreplaceable, and at the same time unmistakably linked to his or her roots.... And for parents each child is original, different, diverse. Allow me to share a family memory. I remember what my mother said about us.... "I have five children." When people asked her: "Which one is your favorite," she answered: "I have five children, like five fingers. [He displays his fingers] Should they strike this one, it hurts me; should they strike that one, it hurts me. All five hurt me. All are my children and all are different like the fingers of a hand."

GENERAL AUDIENCE, PAUL VI AUDIENCE HALL
WEDNESDAY, FEBRUARY 11, 2015

THE MINISTRY OF RAISING CHILDREN

For you Christian parents, the educational mission finds its specific source in the Sacrament of Matrimony, for which the task of raising children is a ministry of the utmost importance in the Church. Not only do parents have a certain educational obligation toward their children, but also children toward their siblings and toward their own parents, meaning that duty of reciprocal help in faith and in goodness. At times it happens that a child is able, with his affection, with his simplicity, to reanimate the entire family.

ADDRESS TO THE ITALIAN CATHOLIC SCOUT MOVEMENT
FOR ADULTS, PAUL VI AUDIENCE HALL
SATURDAY, NOVEMBER 8, 2014

THE WISDOM OF FATHERS

Every family needs a father. Today we shall reflect on the value of his role, and I would like to begin with a few expressions that we find in the Book of Proverbs…. "My son, if your heart is wise, my heart too will be glad. My soul will rejoice when your lips speak what is right" (Pr 23:15–16). Nothing could better express the pride and emotion a father feels when he understands that he has handed down to his child what really matters in life; that is, a wise heart. This father does not say, "I am proud of you because you are the same as me, because you repeat the things I say and do." No, he does not say anything so simple to him. He says something much more important, which we can understand in this way: "I will be happy every time I see you act with wisdom, and I will be moved every time that I hear you speak with righteousness. This is what I wanted to leave to you, that this one thing become yours: the ability to feel and act, to speak and judge, with wisdom and righteousness."

GENERAL AUDIENCE, PAUL VI AUDIENCE HALL
WEDNESDAY, FEBRUARY 4, 2015

THE CHAIN OF FAITH

Jesus did not need to be baptized, but the first theologians say that, with his body, with his divinity, in baptism he blessed all the waters, so that the waters would have the power to confer baptism. And then, before ascending to heaven, Jesus told us to go into all the world to baptize. And from that day forward until today, this has been an uninterrupted chain: people baptize their children, and their children baptize their own, and those children baptize the next generation....

These children, too, are a link in a chain. You parents have a baby boy or girl to baptize, but in some years they will have a child to baptize, or a grandchild.... Such is the chain of faith! What does this mean? I would like to tell you only this: you are those who transmit the faith, the transmitters; you have a duty to hand on the faith to these children. It is the most beautiful inheritance you will leave to them: the faith! Only this. Today, take this thought home with you. We must be transmitters of the faith. Think about this, always think about how to hand on the faith to your children.

HOMILY, ADMINISTRATION OF THE SACRAMENT
OF BAPTISM, SISTINE CHAPEL
SUNDAY, JANUARY 12, 2014

NOURISHED BY THE WORD OF GOD

In order that the family walk well, with trust and hope, it must be nourished with the Word of God. For this reason it is a happy coincidence that precisely today our Pauline brothers and sisters wish to distribute a large number of Bibles, here in the Square and in many other places. Let us thank our Pauline brothers and sisters! They are doing so on the occasion of the centenary of their foundation by Bl. Giacomo Alberione, a great apostle of communication. So today, as the Synod on the Family opens, with the help of the Paulines we can say: a Bible for every family!

You say to me: "But Father, we have two, three of them already...."

But where have you hidden them?...The Bible is not to be placed on a shelf, but to be kept at hand, to be read often, every day, both individually and together, husband and wife, parents and children—maybe in the evening, and especially on Sundays. This way the family grows and walks with the light and power of the Word of God!

ANGELUS, ST. PETER'S SQUARE
SUNDAY, OCTOBER 5, 2014

The Prayer of the Holy Rosary

I would like to recall the importance and beauty of the prayer of the Holy Rosary. Reciting the Hail Mary, we are led to contemplate the mysteries of Jesus, that is, to reflect on the key moments of his life, so that, as with Mary and St. Joseph, he is the center of our thoughts, of our attention and our actions…. Praying together is a precious moment that further strengthens family life, and friendship! Let us learn to pray more in the family and as a family!

GENERAL AUDIENCE, ST. PETER'S SQUARE
WEDNESDAY MAY 2, 2013

Pope Francis @Pontifex · May 3, 2013
"It would be a good idea, during May, for families to say the Rosary together. Prayer strengthens family life."

If Love Is Missing

The life of a family is filled with beautiful moments: rest, meals together, walks in the park or the countryside, visits to grandparents or to a sick person....But if love is missing, joy is missing, nothing is fun. Jesus gives always gives us that love: he is its endless source. In the sacrament he gives us his word and he gives us the bread of life, so that our joy may be complete.

ADDRESS TO PARTICIPANTS IN
THE PILGRIMAGE OF FAMILIES,
ST. PETER'S SQUARE
SATURDAY, OCTOBER 26, 2013

Pope Francis @Pontifex · December 25, 2014

"With Jesus there is true joy."

Rest in the Lord

To hear and accept God's call, to make a home for Jesus, you must be able to rest in the Lord. You must make time each day to rest in the Lord, to pray. To pray is to rest in the Lord.

You may say to me: "Holy Father, I know that; I want to pray, but there is so much work to do! I must care for my children. I have chores in the home; I am too tired even to sleep well."

I know. This may be true, but if we do not pray, we will not know the most important thing of all: God's will for us. And for all our activity, all our busyness, without prayer we will accomplish very little.

ADDRESS TO FAMILIES, MALL OF ASIA ARENA, MANILA
FRIDAY, JANUARY 16, 2015

Do You Play with Your Children?

About trying to reconcile working hours with family time...let me tell you one thing.... When a young mom or dad comes, I ask: "How many children do you have?" and they tell me. And I ask another question, always: "Tell me: do you play with your children?"

Most of them answer: "What are you asking, Father?"

"Yes, yes: do you play? Do you spend time with your children?"

We are losing this capacity, this wisdom of playing with our children. The economic situation pushes us to this, to lose this. Please, spend time with our children!

MEETING WITH THE WORLD OF LABOR AND INDUSTRY,
UNIVERSITY OF MOLISE
SATURDAY, JULY 5, 2014

The Meaning of "Home"

When we say "home," we mean a place of hospitality, a dwelling, or a pleasant human environment; a place where one is at ease and a place of self-discovery; a place of connection to a community or a territory. More profoundly, home is a word with a typically "familiar" flavor that calls to mind the warmth, affection, and love that can be felt in a family. Hence, the home represents the most precious of human treasures: a place of encounter and of relationships among people who, though they may differ in age, culture and history, live together and help one another grow together. For this reason the home is a crucial place: it is where people grow and can be fulfilled, because it is where every person learns to receive and give love.

ADDRESS TO THE MISSIONARIES OF CHARITY,
"DONO DI MARIA" HOMELESS SHELTER
TUESDAY, MAY 21, 2013

IN SAFE HANDS

Do not be afraid! We are frail and we know it, but he is stronger! If you walk with him there is no problem! A child is very frail—I have seen many children today—but if they're with their father, with their mother, they are safe. With the Lord we are safe. Faith grows with the Lord, from the very hand of the Lord; this helps us grow and makes us strong....

When we say "with the Lord," we mean with the Eucharist, with the Bible, with prayer... but also with the family.

ADDRESS TO MEMBERS OF ECCLESIAL MOVEMENTS,
ST. PETER'S SQUARE
SATURDAY, MAY 18, 2013

Pope Francis @Pontifex · Feb 28, 2014

"The Eucharist is essential for us: it is Christ who wishes to enter our lives and fill us with his grace."

In Praise of Mothers

Every human person owes his or her life to a mother, and almost always owes much of what follows in life to her; both in human and in spiritual formation. Yet, despite being highly lauded from a symbolic point of view— many poems, many beautiful things are said poetically of her—the mother is rarely listened to or helped in daily life. She is rarely considered central to society in her role. Rather, the readiness of mothers to make sacrifices for their children often is taken advantage of so as to "save" on social spending....

Perhaps mothers, ready to sacrifice so much for their children and often for others as well, ought to be listened to more. We should understand more about their daily struggle to be efficient at work and attentive and affectionate in the family.... A mother with her children always has problems, always work. I remember there were five of us children at home, and while one was doing one thing, the other wanted to do another, and our poor mama went back and forth from one to another, but she was happy. She gave us so much.

GENERAL AUDIENCE, PAUL VI AUDIENCE HALL
WEDNESDAY, JANUARY 7, 2015

Wisdom in Our Homes

When a mother takes her child aside and gently reproves him, saying: "Don't do this, because…" and explains with great patience, is this the wisdom of God? Yes! It is what the Holy Spirit gives us in life!

Then, in marriage, for example, the two spouses—the husband and wife—argue, and so they don't look at each other, or if they do look at each other, they look at each other with displeasure. Is this the wisdom of God? No!

But if instead one says: "Ah well, the storm has passed, let's make peace," and they begin again and go forward in peace: is this wisdom? [The people answer: Yes!] Now, this is the gift of wisdom. May it come to our homes, may we have it with the children, may it come to us all!

GENERAL AUDIENCE. ST. PETER'S SQUARE
WEDNESDAY, APRIL 9, 2014

ENTRUST YOUR CHILDREN TO GOD

A last thought: for her children a mother is also able to ask and knock at every door, without hesitation. She does so out of love. And I think of how mothers also and especially knock at the door of God's heart! Mothers say so many prayers for their children, especially for the weaker ones, for those in the greatest need or who have gone down dangerous or erroneous paths in life. A few weeks ago I celebrated Mass in the Church of St. Augustine, here in Rome, where the relics of St. Monica, his mother, are preserved. How many prayers that holy mother raised to God for her son, and how many tears she shed! I am thinking of you, dear mothers: how often you pray for your children, never tiring! Continue to pray and to entrust them to God; he has a great heart! Knock at the doors of God's heart with prayers for your children.

GENERAL AUDIENCE, ST. PETER'S SQUARE
WEDNESDAY, SEPTEMBER 18, 2013

THE CONSOLING PRESENCE OF A FATHER

The first need, then, is precisely this: that a father be present in the family. That he be close to his wife, to share everything: joy and sorrow, hope and hardship. And that he be close to his children as they grow—when they play and when they strive, when they are carefree and when they are distressed, when they are talkative and when they are silent, when they are daring and when they are afraid, when they take a wrong step and when they find their path again—a father who is always present. To say "present" is not to say "controlling"! Fathers who are too controlling cancel out their children, they don't let them develop....

Everyone knows that extraordinary parable of the "prodigal son," or better yet of the "merciful father," which we find in the Gospel of Luke in chapter 15 (cf. 15:11–32). What dignity and what tenderness there is in the expectation of that father, who stands at the door of the house waiting for his son to return! Fathers must be patient. Often there is nothing else to do but wait; pray and wait with patience, gentleness, magnanimity and mercy.

GENERAL AUDIENCE, PAUL VI AUDIENCE HALL
WEDNESDAY, FEBRUARY 4, 2015

What Makes Families Strong

All families, we need God: all of us! We need his help, his strength, his blessing, his mercy, his forgiveness. And we need simplicity to pray as a family: simplicity is necessary! Praying the Our Father together, around the table, is not something extraordinary: it's easy. And praying the Rosary together, as a family, is very beautiful and a source of great strength! And also praying for one another! The husband for his wife, the wife for her husband, both together for their children, the children for their grandparents... praying for each other. This is what it means to pray in the family, and it is what makes the family strong: prayer.

HOMILY, "FAMILY DAY," ST. PETER'S SQUARE
SUNDAY, OCTOBER 27, 2013

Pope Francis @Pontifex · July 31, 2014

"May each family rediscover family prayer, which helps to bring about mutual understanding and forgiveness."

THE FAMILY THAT PRAYS TOGETHER

It is in the family that we first learn how to pray. Don't forget: the family that prays together stays together! This is important. There we come to know God, to grow into men and women of faith, and to see ourselves as members of God's greater family—the Church. In the family we learn how to love, to forgive, to be generous and open, not closed and selfish. We learn to move beyond our own needs, to encounter others and share our lives with them. That is why it is so important to pray as a family! So important! That is why families are so important in God's plan for the Church!

ADDRESS TO FAMILIES,
MALL OF ASIA ARENA, MANILA
FRIDAY, JANUARY 16, 2015

JESUS, FONT OF LOVE

Jesus is the inexhaustible font of that love which overcomes every occasion of self-absorption, solitude, and sadness. In your journey as a family, you share so many beautiful moments: meals, rest, housework, leisure, prayer, trips and pilgrimages, and times of mutual support....Nevertheless, if there is no love then there is no joy, and authentic love comes to us from Jesus. He offers us his Word, which illuminates our path; he gives us the Bread of Life which sustains us on our journey.

LETTER TO FAMILIES, FROM THE VATICAN
SUNDAY, FEBRUARY 2, 2014

Pope Francis @Pontifex · January 18, 2015
"How often we forget to dedicate ourselves to that which truly matters! We forget that we are children of God."

KNOTS OF DISOBEDIENCE

When children disobey their parents, we can say that a little "knot" is created. This happens if the child acts with an awareness of what he or she is doing, especially if there is a lie involved. At that moment, they break trust with their parents. You know how frequently this happens! Then the relationship with their parents needs to be purified of this fault; the child has to ask forgiveness so that harmony and trust can be restored.

Something of the same sort happens in our relationship with God when we do not listen to him, when we do not follow his will, when we do concrete things that demonstrate our lack of trust in him—for that is what sin is—and a kind of knot is created deep within us. These knots take away our peace and serenity. They are dangerous, since many knots can form a tangle which gets more and more painful and difficult to undo.

But we know one thing: nothing is impossible for God's mercy! Even the most tangled knots are loosened by his grace.

ADDRESS FOR "MARIAN DAY," ST. PETER'S SQUARE
SATURDAY, OCTOBER 12, 2013

The Perfect Family Does Not Exist

More than anywhere else, the family is where we daily experience our own limits and those of others, the problems great and small entailed in living peacefully with others. A perfect family does not exist. We should not be fearful of imperfections, weakness or even conflict, but rather learn how to deal with them constructively. The family, where we keep loving one another despite our limits and sins, thus becomes a school of forgiveness. Forgiveness is itself a process of communication. When contrition is expressed and accepted, it becomes possible to restore and rebuild the communication which broke down. A child who has learned in the family to listen to others, to speak respectfully and to express his or her view without negating that of others, will be a force for dialogue and reconciliation in society.

MESSAGE FOR 49TH WORLD COMMUNICATIONS DAY,
FROM THE VATICAN
FRIDAY, JANUARY 23, 2015

A Mother's Unfailing Love

When a child grows up and becomes an adult, he chooses his own path, assumes responsibility, stands on his own two feet, and does what he likes. At times, he can go off course, and some accident may occur. But a mother has the patience to continue to accompany her children, always and in every situation. It is the force of her love that impels her to follow her children on their way with discretion and tenderness. Even when they go astray, she always finds a way to understand them, to be close, to help.

In my region, we have a saying: that a mother can "dar la cara." What does this mean? It means that a mother can "put on a brave face" for her children; in other words, she is always compelled to defend them. I am thinking of the mothers who suffer for their children in prison or in difficult situations: they do not question whether or not their children are guilty, they simply keep on loving them. Mothers often suffer humiliation, but they are not afraid, and they never cease to give of themselves.

GENERAL AUDIENCE, ST. PETER'S SQUARE
WEDNESDAY, SEPTEMBER 18, 2013

Healthy Families, Healthy Societies

Healthy families are essential to the life of a society. It gives consolation and hope to see so many large families that welcome children as a gift from God. They know that every child is a blessing. I have heard it said by some that families with many children, and the birth of many children, are one of the causes of poverty. That opinion seems simplistic to me. I can say, we can all say, that the main cause of poverty is an economic system that has removed human beings from the center and set money their place; an economic system that excludes, always excludes—excludes children, the elderly, young people, the unemployed… and that creates the throw-away culture we live in. We are accustomed to seeing people discarded. This is the main cause of poverty, not large families.

GENERAL AUDIENCE, PAUL VI AUDIENCE HALL
WEDNESDAY, JANUARY 21, 2015

Sustained by the Lord's Grace

We cannot ignore the hardship of many families that is due to unemployment, the problem of housing, the practical impossibility of freely choosing their own educational curriculum; the suffering that is also due to internal conflicts within families, to the failures of the conjugal and family experience and to the violence that unfortunately lurks in families and wreaks havoc even in our homes. We owe it to all and wish to be particularly close to them with respect and with a true sense of brotherhood and solidarity. However, we want above all to remember the simple but beautiful and brave testimony of so many families who joyfully live the experience of marriage and parenthood enlightened and sustained by the Lord's grace and fearlessly face even moments of the cross. Lived in union with the Cross of the Lord, the cross does not hinder the path of love but on the contrary can make it stronger and fuller.

MESSAGE TO PARTICIPANTS IN THE
47TH SOCIAL WEEK OF ITALIAN CATHOLICS
FROM THE VATICAN
WEDNESDAY, SEPTEMBER 11, 2013

Pilgrim Families

When you express profound devotion for the Virgin Mary, you are pointing to the highest realization of the Christian life, the one who by her faith and obedience to God's will, and by her meditation on the words and deeds of Jesus, is the Lord's perfect disciple (cf. *Lumen Gentium*, 53). You express this faith, born of hearing the Word of God, in ways that engage the senses, the emotions and the symbols of the different cultures....In doing so you help to transmit it to others, and especially the simple persons whom, in the Gospels, Jesus calls "the little ones." In effect, "journeying together towards shrines, and participating in other demonstrations of popular piety, bringing along your children and engaging other people, is itself a work of evangelization" (*Aparecida Document*, 264). When you visit shrines, when you bring your family, your children, you are engaged in a real work of evangelization.

HOMILY, ST. PETER'S SQUARE
SUNDAY, MAY 5, 2013

Bless All Fathers!

Dear brothers and sisters, Joseph's mission is certainly unique and unrepeatable, because Jesus is absolutely unique. And yet, in his guardianship of Jesus, forming him to grow in age, wisdom and grace, he is a model for every educator—especially every father. St. Joseph is the model of the educator and the dad, the father. I, therefore, entrust to his protection, all parents...and those who have an educational role in the Church and in society.

In a special way, I would like to greet today, on Father's Day, all parents, all fathers: I greet you from the heart! Let's see: are there any fathers in the square? Raise your hands, dads! Look, there are many fathers! Best wishes, best wishes to you on your day! I ask that you may have the grace to be ever closer to your children. Allow them to grow, but be close, be close! They need you—your presence, your closeness, your love. May you be for them as St. Joseph was for Jesus: guardians of their growth in age, wisdom and grace.

GENERAL AUDIENCE, ST. PETER'S SQUARE
WEDNESDAY, MARCH 19, 2014

ST. JOSEPH, PRAY FOR US

I would also like to tell you something very personal. I have great love for St. Joseph, because he is a man of silence and strength. On my table I have an image of St. Joseph sleeping. Even when he is asleep, he is taking care of the Church! Yes! We know that he can do that. So when I have a problem, a difficulty, I write a little note and I put it underneath St. Joseph, so that he can dream about it! In other words I tell him: pray for this problem!

ADDRESS TO FAMILIES,
MALL OF ASIA ARENA, MANILA
FRIDAY, JANUARY 16, 2015

Pope Francis @Pontifex · November 21, 2013

"To be saints is not a privilege for the few, but a vocation for everyone."

SAINTS AT HOME, SAINTS EVERYWHERE!

Many times, we are tempted to think that sainthood is reserved only to those who have the opportunity to break away from daily affairs in order to dedicate themselves exclusively to prayer. But it is not so!

Some think that sanctity is to close your eyes and to look like a holy icon. No! This is not sanctity! Sanctity is something greater, deeper, which God gives us. Indeed, it is precisely in living with love and offering one's own Christian witness in everyday affairs that we are called to become saints....

Are you married? Be a saint by loving and taking care of your husband or your wife, as Christ did for the Church....

Are you a parent or a grandparent? Be a saint by passionately teaching your children or grandchildren to know and to follow Jesus.

It takes so much patience to do this: to be a good parent, a good grandfather, a good mother, a good grandmother; it takes so much patience and with this patience comes holiness: by exercising patience.

GENERAL AUDIENCE, ST. PETER'S SQUARE
WEDNESDAY, NOVEMBER 19, 2014

When Tensions Arise

For most of us, the family is the principal place in which we begin to "breathe" values and ideals, as we develop our full capacity for virtue and charity. At the same time, as we know, in families tensions arise: between egoism and altruism, between reason and passion, between immediate desires and long-term goals, and so on. But families also provide the environment in which these tensions are resolved.

ADDRESS TO PARTICIPANTS IN THE INTERNATIONAL
COLLOQUIUM ON THE COMPLEMENTARITY BETWEEN
MAN AND WOMAN, SYNOD HALL
MONDAY, NOVEMBER 17, 2014

Pope Francis @Pontifex · May 22, 2013

"To live according to the Gospel is to fight against selfishness. The Gospel is forgiveness and peace; it is love that comes from God."

Learn to Say, "I'm Sorry"

In life we err frequently, we make many mistakes. We all do.... We accuse the other to avoid saying "I'm sorry," or "Forgive me." It's an old story! It is an instinct that stands at the origin of so many disasters.

Let us learn to acknowledge our mistakes and to ask for forgiveness: "Forgive me if today I raised my voice." "I'm sorry if I passed without greeting you." "Excuse me if I was late...if this week I was very silent...if I spoke too much without ever listening." "Excuse me; I forgot." "I'm sorry I was angry and I took it out on you."

We can say many "I'm sorrys" every day. In this way, too, a Christian family grows. We all know that the perfect family does not exist, nor a perfect husband or wife.... Don't let a day end without asking forgiveness, without peace returning to our home, to our family.

ADDRESS TO ENGAGED COUPLES PREPARING FOR
MARRIAGE, ST. PETER'S SQUARE
FRIDAY, FEBRUARY 14, 2014

A Mother's Sorrow

Mothers are the strongest antidote to the spread of self-centered individualism. "Individual" means "what cannot be divided." Mothers, instead, "divide" themselves from the moment they bear a child; they help him grow then they give him to the world. It is they, mothers, who most hate war, which kills their children. Many times I have thought of those mothers who receive the letter: "I inform you that your son has fallen in defense of his homeland…." The poor women! How mothers suffer!

GENERAL AUDIENCE, PAUL VI AUDIENCE HALL
WEDNESDAY, JANUARY 7, 2015

Pray Humbly before God

In the light of God's Word, I would like to ask you, dear families: Do you pray together from time to time as a family? Some of you do, I know.

So many people say to me: "But how can we?"

As the tax collector does, it is clear: humbly, before God. All of us, with humility, allowing ourselves to be gazed upon by the Lord and imploring his goodness, that he may visit us.

You may say, "But in the family how is this done? After all, prayer seems to be something personal, and besides there is never a good time, a moment of peace…."

Yes, all that is true enough, but it is also a matter of humility, of realizing that we need God; just like the tax collector.

HOMILY, "FAMILY DAY," ST. PETER'S SQUARE
SUNDAY, OCTOBER 27, 2013

A School for Learning

The family is the privileged school for learning generosity, sharing, responsibility: a school that teaches us how to overcome a certain individualistic mind-set which has worked its way into our society. Sustaining and promoting families, making the most of their fundamental and central role, means working for a just and supportive development.

MESSAGE TO PARTICIPANTS IN THE 47TH SOCIAL WEEK
OF ITALIAN CATHOLICS, FROM THE VATICAN
WEDNESDAY, SEPTEMBER 11, 2013

Pope Francis @Pontifex · May 10, 2014

"A family enlightened by the Gospel provides a school for Christian living! There one learns faithfulness, patience and sacrifice."

A Recipe for Joy

The basis of the feeling of deep joy is the presence of God: the presence of God in the family, and his love—which is welcoming, merciful, and respectful towards all. And above all, a love which is patient. Patience is a virtue of God, and he teaches us how to cultivate it in family life; how to be patient, and lovingly so, with each other. To be patient among ourselves. A patient love. God alone knows how to create harmony from differences. But if God's love is lacking, the family loses its harmony: self-centeredness prevails and joy fades.

HOMILY, "FAMILY DAY," ST. PETER'S SQUARE
SUNDAY, OCTOBER 27, 2013

PRAYER IN MOMENTS OF PAIN

There are many things that we cannot understand. When children begin growing up they do not understand certain things, and they begin to ask their father and mother questions: "Why father? Why? Why?" Psychologists call this the "age of the why"…and if we pay attention we will see that the child does not wait for his father's or mother's response. He will continue to ask why…because the child is insecure and needs his father and mother to look at him. He needs his parents' gaze, he needs the heart of his parents.

In moments of great suffering, do not tire of asking "Why?" as children do…for thus will you draw our Father's eyes to your people; you will draw the affection of our Father in heaven upon you, just like the child who asks, "Why? Why?"

In moments of pain, let this prayer be your strength— the prayer of "Why?"—without asking for explanation, but asking only that our Father watch over us. I am with you in this prayer of "Why?"

ADDRESS TO THE FILIPINO COMMUNITY,
VATICAN BASILICA
THURSDAY, NOVEMBER 21, 2013

Jesus Does Not Disappoint

I am here to tell you that Jesus is Lord; that Jesus does not disappoint....

So many of you have lost everything. I do not know what to tell you. But surely he knows what to tell you! So many of you have lost members of your family. I can only be silent; I accompany you silently, with my heart....

Many of you looked to Christ and asked: "Why, Lord?" To each of you the Lord responds from his heart. I have no other words to say to you. Let us look to Christ: he is the Lord, and he understands us, for he experienced all the troubles we experience.

With him, beneath the cross, is his Mother. We are like that child who stands down there, who, in times of sorrow and pain, times when we understand nothing, times when we want to rebel, can only reach out and cling to her skirts and say to her: "Mother!" Like a little child who is frightened and says: "Mother." Perhaps that is the only word which can express all the feelings we have in those dark moments: Mother!

HOMILY, TACLOBAN INTERNATIONAL AIRPORT
SATURDAY, JANUARY 17, 2015

A Time of Grace

In a special way, old age is a time of grace, in which the Lord renews his call to us. He calls us to safeguard and transmit the faith. He calls us to pray, especially to intercede. He calls us to be close to those in need.... The elderly, and grandparents, have the ability to understand the most difficult of situations: a great ability! And when they pray for these situations, their prayer is strong; it is powerful!

Grandparents who have received the blessing to see their children's children (cf. Ps 128:6) are entrusted with a great responsibility: to transmit their life experience, their family history, the history of a community, of a people; to share wisdom with simplicity, and faith itself—our most precious heritage! Happy are the families who have grandparents close by!

ADDRESS TO THE ELDERLY, ST. PETER'S SQUARE
SUNDAY, SEPTEMBER 28, 2014

Learning from Our Disabled Children

When it comes to the challenges of communication, families who have children with one or more disabilities have much to teach us. A motor, sensory or mental limitation can be a reason for closing in on ourselves, but it can also become, thanks to the love of parents, siblings, and friends, an incentive to openness, sharing and ready communication with all. It can also help schools, parishes and associations to become more welcoming and inclusive of everyone.

MESSAGE FOR 49TH WORLD COMMUNICATIONS DAY,
FROM THE VATICAN
FRIDAY, JANUARY 23, 2015

COME TO ME, FAMILIES!

Dear families, the Lord knows our struggles: he knows them. He knows the burdens we have in our lives. But the Lord also knows our great desire to find joy and rest! Do you remember? Jesus said, "…that your joy may be complete" (cf. Jn 15:11). Jesus wants our joy to be complete! He said this to the apostles and today he says it to us. Here, then, is the first thing I would like to share with you this evening, and it is a saying of Jesus: "Come to me," families from around the world, Jesus says, "and I will give you rest, so that your joy may be complete." Take home this Word of Jesus, carry it in your hearts, and share it with the family. This Word invites us to come to Jesus so that he may give this joy to us and to everyone.

ADDRESS TO PARTICIPANTS IN THE PILGRIMAGE OF
FAMILIES, ST. PETER'S SQUARE
SATURDAY, OCTOBER 26, 2013

THE SORROWFUL ROAD OF EXILE

Today the Gospel presents the Holy Family to us on the sorrowful road of exile, seeking refuge in Egypt. Joseph, Mary and Jesus experienced the tragic fate of refugees, which is marked by fear, uncertainty and unease (cf. Mt 2:13–15; 19–23). Unfortunately, in our own time, millions of families can identify with this sad reality. Almost every day the television and papers carry news of refugees fleeing from hunger, war and other grave dangers, in search of security and a dignified life for themselves and for their families.

Jesus wanted to belong to a family who experienced these hardships, so that no one would feel excluded from the loving closeness of God. The flight into Egypt caused by Herod's threat shows us that God is present where man is in danger, where man is suffering, where he is fleeing, where he experiences rejection and abandonment. But God is also present where man dreams, where he hopes to return in freedom to his homeland, where he plans and chooses life for his family and dignity for himself and his loved ones.

ANGELUS, ST. PETER'S SQUARE
SUNDAY, DECEMBER 29, 2013

WHATEVER YOU DID FOR THE LEAST OF THESE

How hard it is to flee one's home and livelihood! We thank those who have taken care of the homeless, the orphaned and the destitute. Priests, and men and women religious, gave as much as they could. To those of you who housed and fed people seeking safety—in churches, convents, and rectories—and who continue to assist those still struggling, I thank you. You are a credit to the Church. You are the pride of your nation. I personally thank each one of you. For whatever you did for the least of Christ's brothers and sisters, you did for him (cf. Mt 25:41).

HOMILY, TACLOBAN INTERNATIONAL AIRPORT
SATURDAY, JANUARY 17, 2015

Pope Francis @Pontifex · July 8, 2013

"We pray for a heart which will embrace immigrants. God will judge us upon how we have treated the most needy."

GOD WILL NEVER ABANDON YOU

How many difficulties are present in the life of every individual, among our people, in our communities; yet as great as these may seem, God never allows us to be overwhelmed by them. In the face of those moments of discouragement that we experience in life, in our efforts to evangelize or to embody our faith as parents within the family, I would like to say forcefully: Always know in your heart that God is by your side; he never abandons you! Let us never lose hope! Let us never allow it to die in our hearts! The "dragon," evil, is present in our history, but it does not have the upper hand. The one with the upper hand is God, and God is our hope!

HOMILY, 28TH WORLD YOUTH DAY,
SHRINE OF OUR LADY OF APARECIDA, BRAZIL
WEDNESDAY, JULY 24, 2013

THE GREAT MISSION OF EVERY FAMILY

Each Christian family can first of all welcome Jesus, as Mary and Joseph did. Listen to Jesus, speak with him, guard him, protect him, and grow with him in order to improve the world. Let us make room in our heart and in our day for the Lord, as Mary and Joseph also did—and it was not easy. How many difficulties they had to overcome! They were not a superficial family, they were not an unreal family. The family of Nazareth urges us to rediscover the vocation and mission of the family, of every family. What happened in those 30 years in Nazareth, can happen to us too: by seeking to make love and not hate normal; by making mutual help commonplace, not indifference or enmity....

Jesus comes to save the world. And this is the great mission of the family: to make room for Jesus who is coming, and to welcome Jesus in the family and in each member—child, husband, wife, or grandparent.... Jesus is there. Welcome him there, in order that he may grow spiritually in the family. May the Lord grant us this grace!

GENERAL AUDIENCE, ST. PETER'S SQUARE
WEDNESDAY, DECEMBER 17, 2014

LET US GO FORWARD, FAMILIES!

We must ask the Lord to grant us the Holy Spirit and to grant us the gift of wisdom, that wisdom of God that teaches us to see with God's eyes, to feel with God's heart, to speak with God's words. And so, with this wisdom, let us go forward, let us build our family, let us build the Church, and we will all be sanctified.

GENERAL AUDIENCE, ST. PETER'S SQUARE
WEDNESDAY, APRIL 9, 2014

CHAPTER THREE

~ The Promise of Young People ~

St. John Paul II said that the world needs "a new kind of young person," one committed to the highest ideals and eager to build the civilization of love. Be those young persons! Never lose your idealism! Be joyful witnesses to God's love and the beautiful plan he has for us, for this country, and for the world in which we live.

—POPE FRANCIS, JANUARY 18, 2015

A MAGNIFICENT CALLING

Young people want to live life to the fullest. Encountering Christ, letting themselves be caught up in and guided by his love, enlarges the horizons of existence, gives it a firm hope which will not disappoint. Faith is no refuge for the fainthearted, but something which enhances our lives. It makes us aware of a magnificent calling, the vocation of love.

ENCYCLICAL LETTER, *LUMEN FIDEI*, 53
SATURDAY, JUNE 29, 2013

Pope Francis @Pontifex · September 20, 2014

"Dear young people, listen within: Christ is knocking at the door of your heart."

Keep Hope Alive

I would like to speak especially to you young people: be committed to your daily duties, your studies, your work, to relationships of friendship, to helping others. Your future depends on how you live these precious years of your life. Do not be afraid of commitment, of sacrifice, and do not view the future with fear. Keep your hope alive: there is always a light on the horizon.

GENERAL AUDIENCE, ST. PETER'S SQUARE
WEDNESDAY, MAY 1, 2013

Pope Francis @Pontifex · January 4, 2014
"Dear young people, Jesus wants to be your friend, and wants you to spread the joy of this friendship everywhere."

BE APOSTLES OF PEACE

Be apostles of peace and serenity, beginning with your families. Remind your parents, siblings, and peers that it is a beautiful thing to be loved, and that misunderstandings can be overcome. Together with Jesus, everything is possible. This is important: everything is possible. But this word is not a new invention; Jesus said this word when he descended from the Mount of the Transfiguration. What did Jesus say to the father who asked him to heal his child? "Everything is possible for those who have faith." With faith in Jesus, everything can be done, everything is possible.

ADDRESS TO THE CHILDREN OF
ITALIAN CATHOLIC ACTION, CONSISTORY HALL
THURSDAY, DECEMBER 18, 2014

Pope Francis @Pontifex · July 31, 2013
"Dear young friends, it is worth wagering one's life on Christ and on the Gospel, risking everything for great ideals! #Rio2013 #JMJ"

You Are Called to Moral Greatness

You are called, then, to set a good example, an example of integrity. Naturally, in doing this, you will encounter opposition, negativity, discouragement, and even ridicule. But you have received a gift which enables you to rise above those difficulties. It is the gift of the Holy Spirit. If you nurture this gift by daily prayer and draw strength from sharing in the Eucharist, you will be able to achieve that moral greatness to which Jesus calls you. You will also be a compass for those of your friends who are struggling. I think especially of those young people who are tempted to lose hope, to abandon their high ideals, to drop out of school, or to live from day to day on the streets.

So it is essential not to lose your integrity! Not to compromise your ideals! Not to give in to temptations against goodness, holiness, courage and purity! Rise to the challenge!

ADDRESS TO YOUNG PEOPLE,
SANTO TOMÁS UNIVERSITY, MANILA
SUNDAY, JANUARY 18, 2015

LISTEN TO THE LORD

To listen to the Lord, we must learn to contemplate, to feel his constant presence in our lives. We must stop and converse with him, giving him space in prayer. Each of us, even you boys and girls, young people, so many of you here this morning, should ask yourselves: "How much space do I give to the Lord? Do I stop to talk with him?" Ever since we were children, our parents have taught us to start and end the day with a prayer, teaching us to feel that the friendship and the love of God accompanies us. Let us remember the Lord more in our daily life!

GENERAL AUDIENCE, ST. PETER'S SQUARE
WEDNESDAY, MAY 1, 2013

Pope Francis @Pontifex · July 27, 2013

"Dear young friends, learn to pray every day: this is the way to know Jesus and invite him into your lives. #Rio2013 #JMJ"

Grow in Friendship with Christ

Grow in friendship with Christ by listening to his Word. The Lord speaks to us in the depths of our conscience, he speaks to us through Sacred Scripture, he speaks to us in prayer. Learn to stay before him in silence, to read and meditate on the Bible, especially the Gospels, to converse with him every day in order to feel his presence of friendship and love. Here I would like to emphasize the beauty of a simple contemplative prayer, accessible to all, great and small, the educated and those with little education. It is the prayer of the Holy Rosary. In the Rosary we turn to the Virgin Mary so that she may guide us to an ever closer union with her Son Jesus, to bring us into conformity with him, to have his sentiments and to behave like him. Indeed, in the Rosary while we repeat the Hail Mary we meditate on the Mysteries, on the events of Christ's life, so as to know and love him ever better. The Rosary is an effective means for opening ourselves to God, for it helps us to overcome egotism and to bring peace to hearts, to the family, to society and to the world.

MESSAGE TO YOUNG LITHUANIANS, 6TH NATIONAL
YOUTH DAY, FROM THE VATICAN
FRIDAY, JUNE 21, 2013

The Blessing of Baptism

To know the date of our Baptism is to know a blessed day. The danger of not knowing is that we can lose awareness of what the Lord has done in us, the memory of the gift we have received. Thus, we end up considering it only as an event that took place in the past—and not by our own will but by that of our parents—and that it has no impact on the present. We must reawaken the memory of our Baptism.

GENERAL AUDIENCE, ST. PETER'S SQUARE
WEDNESDAY, JANUARY 8, 2014

Pope Francis @Pontifex · February 4, 2014

"Dear young people, Jesus gives us life, life in abundance. If we are close to him we will have joy in our hearts and a smile on our face."

BE JOYFUL LEADERS

To altar servers/teens:

The Lord calls each one of you to work in his field; he calls you to be joyous leaders in his Church, ready to communicate to your friends what he has communicated to you, especially his mercy....

Many teenagers and young people waste too much time in futile activities: chatting on the Internet or on mobile phones and watching "soap operas" on TV. Technological progress should simplify and improve the quality of life, but sometimes it distracts us from what is really important. Among the many things we do in our daily routines, one of the priorities should be to remind ourselves of our Creator who allows us to live, who loves us, and who accompanies us on our journey....

Dear boys and girls, do not misuse your freedom! Do not squander the great dignity of being children of God that has been given to you! If you follow Jesus and his Gospel, your freedom will begin to bud and blossom like a plant in flower and it will bear good and abundant fruit!

ADDRESS TO GERMAN ALTAR SERVERS,
ST. PETER'S SQUARE
TUESDAY, AUGUST 5, 2014

GOD MAKES ALL THINGS NEW

Dear Confirmands,

God is even now making all things new; the Holy Spirit is truly transforming us, and through us he also wants to transform the world in which we live. Let us open the doors to the Spirit, let ourselves be guided by him, and allow God's constant help to make us new men and women, inspired by the love of God which the Holy Spirit bestows on us! How beautiful it would be if each of you, every evening, could say: Today at school, at home, at work, guided by God, I showed a sign of love towards one of my friends, my parents, an older person! How beautiful!

HOMILY, CONFERRAL OF THE
SACRAMENT OF CONFIRMATION,
ST. PETER'S SQUARE
SUNDAY, APRIL 28, 2013

Pope Francis @Pontifex · October 10, 2014

"Dear young people, Christ is counting on you to be his friends and witnesses to his infinite love."

ACTIVATE THE HOLY SPIRIT

When we welcome the Holy Spirit into our hearts and allow him to act, Christ makes himself present in us and takes shape in our lives. Through us, it will be Christ himself who prays, forgives, gives hope and consolation, serves the brethren, draws close to the needy and to the least, creates community, and sows peace. Think how important this is: by means of the Holy Spirit, Christ himself comes to do all this among us and for us. That is why it is important that children and young people receive the Sacrament of Confirmation.

GENERAL AUDIENCE, ST. PETER'S SQUARE
WEDNESDAY, JANUARY 29, 2014

Love Builds a Better World

I wanted in a particular way to meet with young people, to listen to you and to talk with you. I want to express the love and the hopes of the Church for you. And I want to encourage you, as Christian citizens of this country, to offer yourselves passionately and honestly to the great work of renewing your society and helping to build a better world....

One of the greatest challenges young people face is learning to love. To love means to take a risk: the risk of rejection, the risk of being taken advantage of or, worse, the risk of taking advantage of another. Do not be afraid to love! But in love, too, maintain your integrity! Here too be honest and fair!

ADDRESS TO YOUNG PEOPLE,
SANTO TOMÁS UNIVERSITY, MANILA
SUNDAY, JANUARY 18, 2015

Pope Francis @Pontifex · January 27, 2014

"Dear young people, let us not be satisfied with a mediocre life. Be amazed by what is true and beautiful, what is of God!"

The Path of Christian Hope

You and your friends are filled with the optimism, energy and good will which are so characteristic of this period of life. Let Christ turn your natural optimism into Christian hope, your energy into moral virtue, your good will into genuine self-sacrificing love! This is the path you are called to take. This is the path to overcoming all that threatens hope, virtue and love in your lives and in your culture. In this way your youth will be a gift to Jesus and to the world. As young Christians, whether you are workers or students, whether you have already begun a career or have answered the call to marriage, religious life or the priesthood, you are not only a part of the future of the Church; you are also a necessary and beloved part of the Church's *present!*…

Keep close to one another, draw ever closer to God, and with your bishops and priests spend these years in building a holier, more missionary and humble Church…a Church which loves and worships God by seeking to serve the poor, the lonely, the infirm and the marginalized.

HOMILY, 6TH ASIAN YOUTH DAY,
REPUBLIC OF KOREA
MONDAY, AUGUST 18, 2014

God's Enthusiasm in You

The enthusiasm and festive atmosphere which you know how to create are contagious. Enthusiasm is contagious. But do you know where this word comes from—enthusiasm? It comes from Greek and it means "to have something of God inside" or "to be inside God." Enthusiasm, when it is healthy, demonstrates this: that one has something of God inside and expresses him joyously. Be open with this enthusiasm and hope. Yearn for fullness; yearn to give meaning to your future, to your whole life. Yearn to imagine the appropriate journey for each of you and to choose the path that brings you peace and human fulfillment.

ADDRESS TO THE YOUNG PEOPLE
OF ABRUZZI AND MOLISE
CASTELPETROSO CHURCH SQUARE
SATURDAY, JULY 5, 2014

Pope Francis @Pontifex · May 28, 2013
"Dear young people, the Church expects great things of you and your generosity. Don't be afraid to aim high."

THE GREATEST GIFT OF ALL

No matter how much or how little we have individually, each one of us is called to personally reach out and serve our brothers and sisters in need. There is always someone near us who is in need, materially, emotionally, spiritually. The greatest gift we can give to them is our friendship, our concern, our tenderness, our love for Jesus. To receive Jesus is to have everything; to give him is to give the greatest gift of all.

ADDRESS TO YOUNG PEOPLE,
SANTO TOMÁS UNIVERSITY, MANILA
SUNDAY, JANUARY 18, 2015

Pope Francis @Pontifex · November 15, 2013

"Dear young people, always be missionaries of the Gospel, every day and in every place."

Do Not Dilute Your Faith

Please do not water down your faith in Jesus Christ. We dilute fruit drinks—orange, apple, or banana juice—but please do not drink a diluted form of faith. Faith is whole and entire, not something that you water down. It is faith in Jesus. It is faith in the Son of God made man, who loved me and who died for me.

ADDRESS TO THE YOUTH OF ARGENTINA,
28TH WORLD YOUTH DAY, RIO DE JANEIRO
THURSDAY, JULY 25, 2013

THINK BIG!

Dear brothers and sisters, St. John, writing to young people, told them: "You are strong, and the word of God abides in you, and you have overcome the evil one" (1 Jn 2:14). Young people want to live intense experiences! I challenge you: Say no to an ephemeral, superficial and throwaway culture, a culture that assumes that you are not strong, that you are not capable of facing great challenges in your life! Think big!

MESSAGE TO DUTCH YOUNG PEOPLE AT THE
NATIONAL CATHOLIC YOUTH FESTIVAL
SATURDAY, JUNE 28, 2014

A Transcendent Hope

Listen! Young people are the window through which the future enters the world. They are the window, and so they present us with great challenges. Our generation will show that it can rise to the promise found in each young person when we know how to give them space. This means that we have to create the material and spiritual conditions for their full development; to give them a solid basis on which to build their lives; to guarantee their safety and their education to be everything they can be; to pass on to them lasting values that make life worth living; to give them a transcendent horizon for their thirst for authentic happiness and their creativity for the good; to give them the legacy of a world worthy of human life; and to awaken in them their greatest potential as builders of their own destiny, sharing responsibility for the future of everyone. If we can do all this, we anticipate today the future that enters the world through the window of the young.

WELCOME CEREMONY, 28TH WORLD YOUTH DAY,
RIO DE JANEIRO
MONDAY, JULY 22, 2013

Pope Francis @Pontifex · October 5, 2013

"Dear young people, you have many plans and dreams for the future. But, is Christ at the center of each of your plans and dreams?"

You Can Make a Difference

Many of you know what it is to be poor. But many of you have also experienced something of the blessedness that Jesus promised to "the poor in spirit" (cf. Mt 5:3). Here I would say a word of encouragement and gratitude to those of you who choose to follow our Lord in his poverty through a vocation to the priesthood and the religious life; by drawing on that poverty you will enrich many. But to all of you, especially those who can do more and give more, I ask: Please, do more! Please, give more! When you give of your time, your talents and your resources to the many people who struggle and who live on the margins, you make a difference....

ADDRESS TO YOUNG PEOPLE,
SANTO TOMÁS UNIVERSITY, MANILA
SUNDAY, JANUARY 18, 2015

PLAY ALWAYS ON THE OFFENSIVE!

Young people, please: don't put yourselves at the tail end of history. Be active members! Go on the offensive! Play down the field, build a better world, a world of brothers and sisters, a world of justice, of love, of peace, of fraternity, of solidarity. Play always on the offensive!

St. Peter tells us that we are living stones, which form a spiritual edifice (cf. 1 Pet 2:5).... Don't build a little chapel which holds only a small group of persons. Jesus asks us to make his living Church so large that it can hold all of humanity, that it can be a home for everyone! To me, to you, to each of us he says: "Go and make disciples of all nations." Tonight, let us answer him: Yes, Lord, I too want to be a living stone; together we want to build up the Church of Jesus! I want to go forth and build up the Church of Christ!

PRAYER VIGIL WITH THE YOUNG PEOPLE, 28TH WORLD
YOUTH DAY, WATERFRONT OF COPACABANA
SATURDAY, JULY 27, 2013

PRAY WITH ME FOR PEACE

Dear young people, I ask you to join me in praying for peace. You can do this by offering your daily efforts and struggles to God; in this way your prayer will become particularly precious and effective. I also encourage you to assist, through your generosity and sensitivity, in building a society which is respectful of the vulnerable, the sick, children and the elderly. Despite your difficulties in life, you are a sign of hope. You have a place in God's heart, you are in my prayers. I am grateful that so many of you are here, and for your warmth, joy and enthusiasm. Thank you!

ADDRESS TO REFUGEES AND DISABLED YOUNG PEOPLE, LATIN CHURCH, BETHANY BEYOND THE JORDAN SATURDAY, MAY 24, 2014

Pope Francis @Pontifex · July 3, 2014

"Dear young people, do not give up your dreams of a more just world!"

BE GOOD STEWARDS OF CREATION

You are called to care for creation not only as responsible citizens, but also as followers of Christ! Respect for the environment means more than simply using cleaner products or recycling what we use. These are important aspects, but not enough. We need to see, with the eyes of faith, the beauty of God's saving plan, and the link between the natural environment and the dignity of the human person. Men and women are made in the image and likeness of God, and we have been given dominion over creation (cf. Gen 1:26–28). As stewards of God's creation, we are called to make the earth a beautiful garden for the human family. When we destroy our forests, ravage our soil and pollute our seas, we betray that noble calling....

Dear young people, the just use and stewardship of the earth's resources is an urgent task, and you have an important contribution to make.

ADDRESS TO YOUNG PEOPLE,
SANTO TOMÁS UNIVERSITY, MANILA
SUNDAY, JANUARY 18, 2015

The Future Is in Your Hands

Will the future be better or worse? I don't have a wizard's crystal ball to tell the future. But I will tell you one thing: do you know where the future is? It is in your heart. It is in your mind and in your hands. If you feel good, if you think hard, and if you carry forward these good thoughts and good feelings with your hands, the future will be better. The future is for young people. But please note, it is for young people with two qualities: young people with wings and with roots. Young people with wings to fly, dream and create; and young people with roots to receive the wisdom that the elderly give.

The future is in your hands, if you have wings and roots. Have the courage to put on wings, to dream of good things, to dream of a better world, to protest wars. On the other hand, respect the wisdom that you have received from those who are older than you: your parents, your grandparents, the elderly of your country. The future is in your hands. Take the opportunity to make it better.

VIDEO CONFERENCE WITH THE STUDENTS OF THE
SCHOLAS SOCIAL NETWORK, SYNOD HALL
THURSDAY, SEPTEMBER 4, 2014

Do You Listen to Your Grandparents?

Let me ask you: Do you listen to your grandparents? Do you open your hearts to the memories that your grandparents pass on? Grandparents are like the wisdom of the family, they are the wisdom of a people. And a people that does not listen to grandparents is one that dies! Listen to your grandparents.... Every family is part of the history of a people; it cannot exist without the generations who have gone before it.

ADDRESS TO THE PARTICIPANTS IN THE
PILGRIMAGE OF FAMILIES, ST. PETER'S SQUARE
SATURDAY, OCTOBER 26, 2013

KEEP YOUR EYES FIXED ON THE FUTURE

Dear Young People…. May you always keep your eyes fixed on the future. May you be fertile ground on the journey with humanity. May you renew the culture, society and the Church. This takes courage, humility and listening in order to bring about renewal. I entrust you to Blessed Paul VI, that he, in communion with the Saints, may encourage you on your journey and, while I ask you to pray for me, from my heart I bless you!

MESSAGE TO THE ITALIAN CATHOLIC FEDERATION OF
UNIVERSITY STUDENTS, FROM THE VATICAN
TUESDAY, OCTOBER 14, 2014

Pope Francis @Pontifex · August 15, 2014

"Dear young people, Christ asks you to be wide awake and alert, to see the things in life that really matter."

GO AND BUILD A BETTER WORLD!

In a particular way, I wish to greet the young! They say that Albania is the youngest country in Europe and I wish to greet you. I invite you to build your lives on Jesus Christ, on God: the one who builds on God builds on rock, because he is always faithful, even if we sometimes lack faith (cf. 2 Tim. 2:13). Jesus knows us better than anyone else; when we sin, he does not condemn us but rather says to us, "Go and sin no more" (Jn 8:11)....

With the power of the Gospel and the example of your ancestors and the martyrs, you know how to say "No." Say "No" to the idolatry of money, say "No" to the false freedom of individualism, say "No" to addiction and to violence.

You also know how to say "Yes." Say "Yes" to a culture of encounter and of solidarity, say "Yes" to the beauty that is inseparable from the good and the true, say "Yes" to a life lived with great enthusiasm and at the same time faithful in little things.

ANGELUS, TIRANA (ALBANIA)
SUNDAY, SEPTEMBER 21, 2014

CHAPTER FOUR

~ The Vocation and Mission of the Family ~

The family which experiences the joy of faith communicates it naturally. That family is the salt of the earth and the light of the world, it is the leaven of society as a whole. Dear families, always live in faith and simplicity, like the Holy Family of Nazareth! The joy and peace of the Lord be always with you!

HOMILY, "FAMILY DAY," ST. PETER'S SQUARE
SUNDAY, OCTOBER 27, 2013

THE FAMILY—A DRIVING FORCE IN THE WORLD

One could say, without exaggeration, that the family is the driving force of the world and of history. Our personality develops in the family, by growing up with our mom and dad, our brothers and sisters, by breathing in the warmth of the home. The family is the place where we receive our name, it is the place of affection, the space of intimacy, where one acquires the art of dialogue and interpersonal communication. In the family the person becomes aware of his or her own dignity and, especially if their upbringing is Christian, each one recognizes the dignity of every single person, in a particular way the sick, the weak and the marginalized.

The family-community is all of this and it needs to be recognized as such, and more urgently today when the protection of individual rights prevail. And we must defend the right of this community: the family.

ADDRESS TO THE PONTIFICAL COUNCIL FOR THE FAMILY,
CLEMENTINE HALL
FRIDAY, OCTOBER 25, 2013

A BLESSING FOR ALL OF HUMANITY

With Mary, Joseph served as a model for the boy Jesus as he grew in wisdom, age and grace (cf. Lk 2:52). When families bring children into the world, train them in faith and sound values, and teach them to contribute to society, they become a blessing in our world. Families can become a blessing for all of humanity! God's love becomes present and active by the way we love and by the good works that we do; we extend Christ's kingdom in this world. And in doing this, we prove faithful to the prophetic mission which we have received in baptism.

ADDRESS TO FAMILIES,
MALL OF ASIA ARENA, MANILA
FRIDAY, JANUARY 16, 2015

Pope Francis @Pontifex · January 16, 2015

"The family is the greatest treasure of any country. Let us all work to protect and strengthen this, the cornerstone of society."

THE GOSPEL OF THE FAMILY

The "Good News" of the family is a very important part of evangelization, which Christians can communicate to all, by the witness of their lives. Already they are doing so; this is evident in secularized societies. Truly Christian families are known by their fidelity, their patience, their openness to life, and their respect for the elderly...the secret to this is the presence of Jesus in the family. Let us therefore propose to all people, with respect and courage, the beauty of marriage and the family illuminated by the Gospel! And in order to do this let us approach with care and affection those families who are struggling, forced to leave their homeland, broken, homeless or unemployed, or suffering for any reason; let us approach married couples in crisis or separated. Let us be close to everyone through the proclamation of this Gospel of the family, the beauty of the family.

ADDRESS TO THE PONTIFICAL COUNCIL
FOR THE FAMILY, CLEMENTINE HALL
FRIDAY, OCTOBER 25, 2013

How Do I Bear Witness?

We should all ask ourselves: How do I bear witness to Christ through my faith? Do I have the courage of Peter and the other Apostles, to think, to choose and to live as a Christian, obedient to God? To be sure, the testimony of faith comes in very many forms; just as in a great fresco there is a variety of colors and shades, all of which are important, even those that do not stand out. In God's great plan, every detail is important: your witness, my humble little witness, even the hidden witness of those who live their faith with simplicity in everyday family relationships, work relationships, and friendships. These are the saints of every day, the "hidden" saints, a sort of "middle class of holiness," as a French author said, that "middle class of holiness" to which we all can belong.

HOMILY, BASILICA OF ST. PAUL OUTSIDE-THE-WALLS
SUNDAY, APRIL 14, 2013

Pope Francis @Pontifex · December 28, 2014

"The Christian family is missionary: it announces the love of God to the world."

RISE FROM YOUR SLUMBER!

Once we have heard God's voice, we must rise from our slumber; we must get up and act (cf. Rom 13:11). In our families, we have to get up and act! Faith does not remove us from the world, but draws us more deeply into it. This is very important! We have to be deeply engaged with the world, but with the power of prayer. Each of us, in fact, has a special role in preparing for the coming of God's kingdom in our world.

ADDRESS TO FAMILIES,
MALL OF ASIA ARENA, MANILA
FRIDAY, JANUARY 16, 2015

Do Not Be Divided by Passing Ideologies

In these days, as you reflect on the complementarity between man and woman, I urge you to emphasize yet another truth about marriage: that the permanent commitment to solidarity, fidelity and fruitful love responds to the deepest longings of the human heart. Let us think especially of the young people who represent our future: it is important that they should not let the harmful mentality of the temporary affect them, but rather that they be revolutionaries with the courage to seek strong and lasting love, in other words, to go against the current. This must be done.

I would like to say one thing about this: we must not fall into the trap of being limited by ideological concepts. The family is an anthropological fact, and consequently a social, cultural fact, etc. We cannot qualify it with ideological concepts which are compelling at only one moment in history and then decline. Today there can be no talk of the conservative family or the progressive family: family is family! Do not allow yourselves to be qualified by these ideologies or by other ideological concepts. The family has a force of its own.

ADDRESS TO PARTICIPANTS IN THE INTERNATIONAL
COLLOQUIUM ON THE COMPLEMENTARITY BETWEEN
MAN AND WOMAN, SYNOD HALL
MONDAY, NOVEMBER 17, 2014

The Bricks That Build Up Society

It is impossible to quantify the strength and depth of humanity contained in a family: mutual help, educational support, relationships developing as family members mature, the sharing of joys and difficulties. Families are the first place in which we are formed as persons and, at the same time, the "bricks" for the building up of society.

HOMILY, ST. PETER'S SQUARE
SUNDAY, SEPTEMBER 14, 2014

Pope Francis @Pontifex · October 23, 2014

"The family is where we are formed as people. Every family is a brick in the building of society."

THREATS TO THE FAMILY

The pressures on family life today are many.... While all too many people live in dire poverty, others are caught up in materialism and lifestyles which are destructive of family life and the most basic demands of Christian morality. These are forms of ideological colonization. The family is also threatened by growing efforts on the part of some to redefine the very institution of marriage, by relativism, by the culture of the ephemeral, by a lack of openness to life.

I think of Blessed Paul VI. At a time when the problem of population growth was being raised, he had the courage to defend openness to life in families. He knew the difficulties that are there in every family, and so in his encyclical he was very merciful towards particular cases, and he asked confessors to be very merciful and understanding in dealing with particular cases. But he also had a broader vision: he looked at the peoples of the earth and he saw this threat of families being destroyed for lack of children.

ADDRESS TO FAMILIES,
MALL OF ASIA ARENA, MANILA
FRIDAY, JANUARY 16, 2015

POVERTY OF THE HEART

In many societies, we are experiencing a profound poverty of relationships as a result of the lack of solid family and community relationships. We are concerned by the various types of hardship, marginalization, isolation, and various forms of pathological dependencies which we see increasing. This kind of poverty can be overcome only through the rediscovery and valuing of fraternal relationships in the heart of families and communities, through the sharing of joys and sorrows, and of the hardships and triumphs that are a part of human life.

MESSAGE FOR 2014 WORLD DAY OF PEACE,
FROM THE VATICAN
SUNDAY, DECEMBER 8, 2013

Pope Francis @Pontifex · December 30, 2014

"Today people are suffering from poverty, but also from lack of love."

RESIST THE CULTURE OF THE TEMPORARY

Marriage and the family are in crisis today. We now live in a culture of the temporary, in which more and more people reject marriage as a public obligation. This revolution of customs and morals has often waved "the flag of freedom," but it has, in reality, brought spiritual and material devastation to countless human beings, especially the poorest and most vulnerable. It is ever more evident that the decline of the culture of marriage is associated with increased poverty and a host of other social ills that disproportionately affect women, children and the elderly. It is always they who suffer the most in this crisis.

ADDRESS TO PARTICIPANTS IN THE INTERNATIONAL COLLOQUIUM ON THE COMPLEMENTARITY BETWEEN MAN AND WOMAN, SYNOD HALL
MONDAY, NOVEMBER 17, 2014

Pope Francis @Pontifex · June 16, 2014

"May the Lord bless the family and strengthen it in this moment of crisis."

A Just and Redeemed Social Order

The Gospel is the promise of God's grace, which alone can bring wholeness and healing to our broken world. It can inspire the building of a truly just and redeemed social order....

The Gospel calls individual Christians to live lives of honesty, integrity and concern for the common good. But it also calls Christian communities to create "circles of integrity," networks of solidarity which can expand to embrace and transform society by their prophetic witness....

Proclaim the beauty and truth of the Christian message to a society which is tempted by confusing presentations of sexuality, marriage and the family. As you know, these realities are increasingly under attack from powerful forces which threaten to disfigure God's plan for creation and betray the very values which have inspired and shaped all that is best in your culture.

HOMILY, CATHEDRAL OF THE IMMACULATE
CONCEPTION, MANILA
FRIDAY, JANUARY 16, 2015

THE FAMILY IN CRISIS

The family is experiencing a profound cultural crisis, as are all communities and social bonds. In the case of the family, the weakening of these bonds is particularly serious because the family is the fundamental cell of society, where we learn to live with others despite our differences and to belong to one another; it is also the place where parents pass on the faith to their children. Marriage now tends to be viewed as a form of mere emotional satisfaction that can be constructed in any way or modified at will. But the indispensible contribution of marriage to society transcends the feelings and momentary needs of the couple. As the French bishops have taught, it is not born "of loving sentiment, ephemeral by definition, but from the depth of the obligation assumed by the spouses who accept to enter a total communion of life."

APOSTOLIC EXHORTATION, *EVANGELII GAUDIUM*, 66
NOVEMBER 24, 2013

Pope Francis @Pontifex · January 16, 2015
"The family is the greatest treasure of any country. Let us all work to protect and strengthen this, the cornerstone of society."

Be Sanctuaries of Respect for Life

The future passes through the family. So protect your families! Protect your families! See in them your country's greatest treasure and nourish them always by prayer and the grace of the sacraments. Families will always have their trials, but may you never add to them! Instead, be living examples of love, forgiveness and care. Be sanctuaries of respect for life, proclaiming the sacredness of every human life from conception to natural death. What a gift this would be to society, if every Christian family lived fully its noble vocation! So rise with Jesus and Mary, and set out on the path the Lord traces for each of you.

ADDRESS TO FAMILIES,
MALL OF ASIA ARENA, MANILA
FRIDAY, JANUARY 16, 2015

BUILDING INCLUSIVE SOCIETIES

We Christians, together with all people of good will, are called to patiently build a more diverse, more welcoming, more humane, and more inclusive society that does not need to discard those who are weak in body and mind. On the contrary we need a society which measures its success on how the weak are cared for.

As Christians and as citizens, we are called to envision, with imagination and wisdom, ways of facing this challenge. A people who does not take care of grandparents, who does not treat them well has no future! Why does it have no future? Because such a people loses its memory and is torn from its roots. But beware: it is your responsibility to keep these roots alive in yourselves with prayer, by reading the Gospel and through works of mercy. In this way we will remain as living trees that even in old age will not stop bearing fruit. One of the most beautiful aspects of family life—of our human life as a family—is caressing a baby and being caressed by a grandfather and a grandmother.

ADDRESS TO THE ELDERLY, ST. PETER'S SQUARE
SUNDAY, SEPTEMBER 28, 2014

Helping Families Live in a Media Environment

Today the modern media, which are an essential part of life for young people in particular, can be both a help and a hindrance to communication in and between families. The media can be a hindrance if they become a way to avoid listening to others, to evade physical contact, to fill up every moment of silence and rest.... The media can help communication when they enable people to share their stories, to stay in contact with distant friends, to thank others or to seek their forgiveness, and to open the door to new encounters. By growing daily in our awareness of the vital importance of encountering others, these "new possibilities," we will employ technology wisely, rather than letting ourselves be dominated by it. Here too, parents are the primary educators, but they cannot be left to their own devices. The Christian community is called to help them in teaching children how to live in a media environment in a way consonant with the dignity of the human person and service of the common good.

MESSAGE FOR 49TH WORLD COMMUNICATIONS DAY,
FROM THE VATICAN
FRIDAY, JANUARY 23, 2015

FAMILIES FOSTER HOPE

The family—united, fruitful and indissoluble—possesses the fundamental elements for fostering hope in the future. Without this solid basis the future ends up being built on sand, with dire social consequences. Then too, stressing the importance of the family not only helps to give direction and hope to new generations, but also to many of our elderly who are often forced to live alone and are effectively abandoned because there is no longer the warmth of a family hearth able to accompany and support them.

ADDRESS TO THE EUROPEAN PARLIAMENT,
STRASBOURG, FRANCE
TUESDAY, NOVEMBER 25, 2014

Pope Francis @Pontifex · June 26, 2014

"The family is essential to sustaining human and social development."

LET PEACE BEGIN AT HOME

Today, from every corner of the globe, believers offer up
their prayers asking the Lord for the gift of peace and the
ability to bring it into every environment. On this first
day of the year, may the Lord help us all to set out more
decisively on the path of justice and peace. And let us begin
at home! Justice and peace at home, among ourselves. It
begins at home and then goes out to all humanity. But we
have to begin at home. May the Holy Spirit act in hearts,
may he melt obstacles and hardness and grant that we may
be moved before the weakness of the Baby Jesus. Peace,
in fact, requires the strength of meekness, the nonviolent
strength of truth and love.

ANGELUS, 47TH WORLD DAY OF PEACE,
ST. PETER'S SQUARE
WEDNESDAY, JANUARY 1, 2014

God's Loving Plan

The Book of Genesis tells us that God created man and woman and entrusted to them the task of filling the earth and subduing it—which does not mean exploiting it, but rather nurturing and protecting it, and caring for it through their work (cf. Gen 1:28; 2:15). Work is part of God's loving plan: we are called to cultivate and care for all the goods of creation. In this way we all share in the work of creation!

Work is fundamental to the dignity of a person. Work, to use a metaphor, "anoints" us with dignity; it fills us with dignity and makes us similar to God, who has worked and still works, and who always acts (cf. Jn 5:17). Work gives us the ability to maintain ourselves and our families, and to contribute to the growth of our nations.

GENERAL AUDIENCE, ST. PETER'S SQUARE
WEDNESDAY, MAY 1, 2013

Pope Francis @Pontifex · November 11, 2014

"Work is so important for human dignity, for building up a family, for peace!"

CHRISTIAN FAMILIES ARE MISSIONARY FAMILIES

How do we keep our faith as a family? Do we keep it for ourselves, in our families, as a personal treasure like a bank account? Or are we able to share it by our witness, by our acceptance of others, by our openness?

We all know that families, especially young families, are often "racing" from one place to another, with lots to do. But did you ever think that this "racing" could also be the race of faith? Christian families are missionary families. Yesterday in this square we heard the testimonies of missionary families. They are missionary also in everyday life, in their doing everyday things, as they bring to everything the salt and the leaven of faith!

HOMILY, "FAMILY DAY," ST. PETER'S SQUARE
SUNDAY, OCTOBER 27, 2013

PROCLAIMING THE LOVE OF GOD

The mission of the Christian family, today as yesterday, is that of proclaiming to the world, by the power of the Sacrament of Marriage, the love of God. From this very proclamation a living family is born and built, one which sets the hearth of love at the center of its human and spiritual dynamism. If, as St. Irenaeus said "Gloria Dei vivens homo" ["The glory of God is man fully alive"]... then a family, which by the grace of God fully lives its vocation, also glorifies God.

LETTER FOR THE 8TH WORLD MEETING OF FAMILIES,
FROM THE VATICAN
TUESDAY, DECEMBER 9, 2014

Pope Francis @Pontifex · December 28, 2014

"The Christian family is missionary: it announces the love of God to the world."

BE MISSIONARY DISCIPLES OF JESUS

During this year which your bishops have set aside as the Year of the Poor, I would ask you, as families, to be especially mindful of our call to be missionary disciples of Jesus. This means being ready to go beyond your homes to care for our brothers and sisters who are most in need. I ask you especially to show concern for those who do not have a family of their own, in particular those who are elderly and children without parents. Never let them feel isolated, alone and abandoned, but help them to know that God has not forgotten them.

Today I was very moved when, after Mass, I visited a home for children without families. How many people work in the Church to make that home a family! This is what it means, in a prophetic sense, to build a family.

You may be poor yourselves in material ways, but you have an abundance of gifts to offer when you offer Christ and the community of his Church. Do not hide your faith, do not hide Jesus, but carry him into the world and offer the witness of your family life!

ADDRESS TO FAMILIES,
MALL OF ASIA ARENA, MANILA
FRIDAY, JANUARY 16, 2015

GO, FOR I AM WITH YOU

I am now going to say something I have already said many times before, but it comes from the heart. Whenever we Christians are enclosed in our groups, our movements, our parishes, in our little worlds, we remain closed, and the same thing happens to us that happens to anything closed: when a room is closed, it begins to get dank. If a person is closed up in that room, he or she becomes ill! Whenever Christians are enclosed in their groups, parishes, or movements, they take ill....

But careful! Jesus does not say: Go off and do things on your own. No! That is not what he is saying. Jesus says: Go, for I am with you! This is what is so beautiful for us; it is what guides us. If we go out to bring his Gospel with love, with a true apostolic spirit, with *parrhesia* [bold, straightforward speech], he walks with us, he goes ahead of us, he gets there first....

ADDRESS TO PARTICIPANTS IN THE PILGRIMAGE OF
CATECHISTS, PAUL VI AUDIENCE HALL
FRIDAY, SEPTEMBER 27, 2013

Be a Breath of Fresh Air!

Dear brothers and sisters, the Church loves you! Be an active presence in the community, as living cells, as living stones.... Love the Church! Let yourselves be guided by her! In your parishes, in your dioceses, be a true "lung" of faith and Christian life, a breath of fresh air! In this square I see a great variety. Earlier on it was a variety of umbrellas, and now it is a variety of colors and signs. This is also the case with the Church: we have a great wealth and variety of expressions. And everything leads back to unity; the variety leads back to unity, and unity is the encounter with Christ.

HOMILY, ST. PETER'S SQUARE
SUNDAY, MAY 5, 2013

A Round of Applause for Mothers!

A society without mothers would be a dehumanized society, for mothers are always, even in the worst moments, witnesses of tenderness, dedication and moral strength. Mothers often pass on the deepest sense of religious practice: in a human being's life, the value of faith is inscribed in the first prayers, the first acts of devotion learned in childhood. It is a message that believing mothers are able to pass on without much explanation: these explanations come later, but the seed of faith is planted in those early precious moments. Without mothers, not only would there be no new faithful, but the faith would lose a good part of its simple and profound warmth....

Dearest mothers, thank you, thank you for what you are in your family and for what you give to the Church and the world...for all the mammas present here: Let us salute them with a round of applause!

GENERAL AUDIENCE,
PAUL VI AUDIENCE HALL
WEDNESDAY, JANUARY 7, 2015

Protect Your Children and Your Families

Sadly, in our day, the family all too often needs to be protected against insidious attacks and programs contrary to all that we hold true and sacred, all that is most beautiful and noble in our culture.

Specifically, we need to see each child as a gift to be welcomed, cherished and protected. And we need to care for our young people, not allowing them to be robbed of hope and condemned to life on the streets.

It was a frail child, in need of protection, who brought God's goodness, mercy and justice into the world. He resisted the dishonesty and corruption which are the legacy of sin, and he triumphed over them by the power of his cross.

HOMILY, RIZAL PARK, MANILA
SUNDAY, JANUARY 18, 2015

INSTRUMENTS OF GOD'S MERCY

The mission that awaits us is of course challenging, but with the guidance of the Holy Spirit it becomes an exciting one. We all experience our poverty and weakness in taking the precious treasure of the Gospel to the world, but we must constantly repeat St Paul's words: "We have this treasure in earthen vessels, to show that the transcendent power belongs to God and not to us" (2 Cor 4:7). It is this that must always give us courage: knowing that the power of evangelization comes from God, that it belongs to him. We are called to open ourselves more and more to the action of the Holy Spirit, to offer our unreserved readiness to be instruments of God's mercy, of his tenderness, of his love for every man and every woman—and especially for the poor, the outcast and those who are distant...

As St Paul said: "If I preach the gospel, that gives me no ground for boasting. For necessity is laid upon me. Woe to me if I do not preach the gospel!" (1 Cor 9:16). God's salvation is for everyone!

ADDRESS TO THE PONTIFICAL MISSION SOCIETIES,
CLEMENTINE HALL
FRIDAY, MAY 17, 2013

FAMILIES: A MORAL GLUE IN SOCIETY

A fundamental role in the renewal of society is played, of course, by the family and especially by young people.... Families have an indispensable mission in society. It is in the family that children are trained in sound values, high ideals and genuine concern for others. But like all God's gifts, the family can also be disfigured and destroyed. It needs our support. We know how difficult it is for our democracies today to preserve and defend such basic human values as respect for the inviolable dignity of each human person, respect for the rights of conscience and religious freedom, and respect for the inalienable right to life, beginning with that of the unborn and extending to that of the elderly and infirm. For this reason, families and local communities must be encouraged and assisted in their efforts to transmit to our young the values and the vision which can help bring about a culture of integrity— one which honors goodness, truthfulness, fidelity and solidarity as the firm foundation and the moral glue which holds society together.

ADDRESS TO DIPLOMATIC CORPS, MALACAÑANG
PRESIDENTIAL PALACE, MANILA
FRIDAY, JANUARY 16, 2015

WE ARE RESPONSIBLE FOR THE WORLD

Today no one in our world feels responsible; we have lost a sense of responsibility for our brothers and sisters. We have fallen into the hypocrisy of the priest and the Levite whom Jesus described in the parable of the Good Samaritan. We see our brother half dead on the side of the road, and perhaps we say to ourselves, "Poor soul!" but then we continue on our way. We feel it's not our responsibility, and with that we feel reassured, assuaged.

The culture of comfort, which makes us think only of ourselves, makes us insensitive to the cries of other people. It makes us live in soap bubbles which, however lovely, are insubstantial; they offer a fleeting and empty illusion which results in indifference to others. Indeed, it even leads to the globalization of indifference. In this globalized world, we have fallen into globalized indifference. We have become used to the suffering of others and say, "It doesn't affect me. It doesn't concern me. It's none of my business!"...

"Adam, where are you?" "Where is your brother?" These are the two questions which God asks at the dawn of human history, and which he also asks each man and woman in our own day, which he also asks us.

HOMILY, SALINA QUARTER, LAMPEDUSA
MONDAY, JULY 8, 2013

PROTECT ONE ANOTHER

The vocation of being a "protector"…is not just something involving us Christians alone; it also has a prior dimension which is simply human, involving everyone…. It means protecting people, showing loving concern for each and every person, especially children, the elderly, and those in need, who are often the last we think about. It means caring for one another in our families: husbands and wives first protect one another, and then, as parents, they care for their children, and children themselves, in time, protect their parents. It means building sincere friendships in which we protect one another in trust, respect, and goodness. In the end, everything has been entrusted to our protection, and all of us are responsible for it. Be protectors of God's gifts!

HOMILY, ST. PETER'S SQUARE
TUESDAY, MARCH 19, 2013

Pope Francis @Pontifex · January 7, 2014
"Let us leave a spare place at our table: a place for those who lack the basics, who are alone."

ABSENT FATHERS

"Father" is a term familiar to everyone, a universal word. It indicates a fundamental relationship, the reality of which is as old as human history. Today, however, some have reached the point of claiming that our society is a "society without fathers." In other words, particularly in Western culture, the father figure is symbolically absent, gone, removed…. On this common journey of reflection on the family, I would like to say to all Christian communities that we must be more attentive: the absent father figure in the life of little ones and young people causes gaps and wounds that may be very serious. And, in effect, delinquency among children and adolescents can be largely attributed to this lack, to the shortage of role models and authoritative guidance in their everyday life, a shortage of closeness, a shortage of love from the father. And the feeling of orphanhood that so many young people live with is more profound than we think.

GENERAL AUDIENCE, PAUL VI AUDIENCE HALL
WEDNESDAY, JANUARY 28, 2015

FORGIVE US, LORD!

We are a society which has forgotten how to weep, how to experience compassion and "suffering with" others: the globalization of indifference has taken from us the ability to weep! In the Gospel we have heard the crying, the wailing, the great lamentation: "Rachel weeps for her children...because they are no more." Herod sowed death to protect his own comfort, his own soap bubble. And so it continues.... Let us ask the Lord to remove the part of Herod that lurks in our hearts. Let us ask the Lord for the grace to weep over our indifference, to weep over the cruelty of our world, of our own hearts, and of all those who in anonymity make social and economic decisions which open the door to tragic situations like this. Has anyone wept? Today has anyone wept in our world?

Lord, in this liturgy, a penitential liturgy, we beg forgiveness for our indifference to so many of our brothers and sisters. Father, we ask your pardon for those who are complacent and closed amid comforts which have deadened their hearts. We beg your forgiveness for those who by their decisions on the global level have created situations that lead to these tragedies. Forgive us, Lord!

HOMILY, SALINA QUARTER, LAMPEDUSA
MONDAY, JULY 8, 2013

WHERE DOES JESUS SEND US?

Where does Jesus send us? There are no borders, no limits: he sends us to everyone. The Gospel is for everyone, not just for some. It is not only for those who seem closer to us, more receptive, and more welcoming. It is for everyone. Do not be afraid to go and to bring Christ into every area of life, to the fringes of society, even to those who seem farthest away or most indifferent. The Lord seeks all, he wants everyone to feel the warmth of his mercy and his love.

PRAYER VIGIL WITH THE YOUNG PEOPLE,
28TH WORLD YOUTH DAY,
WATERFRONT OF COPACABANA
SATURDAY, JULY 27, 2013

Pope Francis @Pontifex · January 17, 2015
"We who are Christians, members of God's family, are called to go out to the needy and to serve them."

GO TO THE OUTSKIRTS

In the Bible, the Lord says: I am like the flower of the almond. Why? Because that is the first flower to blossom in the spring. He is always the first! This is fundamental for us: God is always ahead of us! When we think about going far away, to an extreme outskirt, we may be a bit afraid, but in fact God is already there. Jesus is waiting for us in the hearts of our brothers and sisters, in their wounded bodies, in their hardships, in their lack of faith. But can I tell you about one of the "outskirts" which breaks my heart? I saw it in my first diocese. It is children who don't even know how to make the sign of the cross. In Buenos Aires there are many children who can't make the sign of the cross. This is one of the "outskirts"! And Jesus is there, waiting for you to help that child to make the sign of the cross. He's always there first....

Let us go forth and open doors. Let us have the audacity to mark out new paths for proclaiming the Gospel.

ADDRESS TO PARTICIPANTS IN THE PILGRIMAGE OF
CATECHISTS, PAUL VI AUDIENCE HALL
FRIDAY, SEPTEMBER 27, 2013

Pope Francis @Pontifex · January 5, 2015

"Lord, help us to recognize you in the sick, poor and suffering."

DO NOT BE A CLOSED CHURCH

The Church must step outside herself.... Jesus tells us: "Go into all the world! Go! Preach! Bear witness to the Gospel!" (cf. Mk 16:15). But what happens if we step outside ourselves? The same as can happen to anyone who comes out of the house and onto the street: an accident. But I tell you, I far prefer a Church that has had a few accidents to a Church that has fallen sick from being closed.

ADDRESS TO MEMBERS OF ECCLESIAL MOVEMENTS,
ST. PETER'S SQUARE
SATURDAY, MAY 18, 2013

FAITHFUL, FRUITFUL LOVE

Relationships based on faithful love until death—like marriage, parenthood, or that of siblings—are learned and lived in the household. When these relationships form the basic fabric of a human society, they lend cohesion and consistency. It is therefore not possible to be part of a people, to feel like a neighbor, to take care of someone who is more distant and unfortunate if, in the heart of man, these fundamental relationships which give him security in openness toward others are broken.

Moreover, family love is fruitful, and not only because it generates new life, but because it broadens the horizon of existence. It creates a new world; it makes us believe, despite any discouragement and defeatism, that coexistence based on respect and trust is possible. In facing a materialistic view of the world, the family does not reduce man to sterile utilitarianism, but offers a channel for the realization of his loftiest aspirations.

MESSAGE TO THE FIRST LATIN AMERICAN CONGRESS ON
THE PASTORAL CARE OF THE FAMILY,
FROM THE VATICAN
THURSDAY, MAY 8, 2014

BEAR WITNESS TO THE GOSPEL

All of us are God's children, members of God's family. Today St. Paul has told us that in Christ we have become God's adopted children, brothers and sisters in Christ. This is who we are. This is our identity....

God chose and blessed us for a purpose: to be holy and blameless in his sight (Eph 1:4). He chose us, each of us, to be witnesses of his truth and his justice in this world. He created the world as a beautiful garden and asked us to care for it. But through sin, man has disfigured that natural beauty; through sin, man has also destroyed the unity and beauty of our human family, creating social structures which perpetuate poverty, ignorance and corruption.

Sometimes, when we see the troubles, difficulties and wrongs all around us, we are tempted to give up. It seems that the promises of the Gospel do not apply; they are unreal. But the Bible tells us that the great threat to God's plan for us is, and always has been, the lie. The devil is the father of lies. often he hides his snares behind the appearance of sophistication, the allure of being "modern," or "like everyone else." He distracts us with the view of ephemeral pleasures, superficial pastimes. And so we squander our God-given gifts by tinkering with gadgets. We squander our money on gambling and drink. We turn in on ourselves, forgetting to remain focused on the things that really matter. We forget to remain, at heart, children of God. That is sin: to forget, in our heart, to be children of God.

HOMILY, RIZAL PARK, MANILA
SUNDAY, JANUARY 18, 2015

Pope Francis @Pontifex · January 16, 2014

Let us pray for peace, and let us bring it about, starting in our own homes!

THE ROOT OF PEACE

Peace is not simply the absence of war, but a general condition in which the human person is in harmony with him/herself, in harmony with nature and in harmony with others....

Let us recall, here in the square, that sign: "Prayer is at the root of peace." This gift must be implored and must be welcomed with commitment every day, in whatever situation we are in. At the dawn of this new year, we are all called to rekindle in our heart an impulse of hope, which must be translated into concrete works of peace.

Are you in disaccord with someone? Make peace!

Are you in disaccord at home? Make peace!

Are you in disaccord in your community? Make peace!

Are you in disaccord at your place of work? Make peace!

Work for peace, reconciliation and fraternity. Each of us must perform gestures of fraternity toward our neighbor, especially toward those who are tried by family tensions or various types of conflict. These small gestures are of so much value: they can be seeds which give hope, and they can open paths and perspectives of peace.

ANGELUS, ST. PETER'S SQUARE
SUNDAY, JANUARY 4, 2015

Weep for Our Children

Sadly, in this world, with all its highly developed technology, great numbers of children continue to live in inhuman situations, on the fringes of society, in the peripheries of great cities and in the countryside. All too many children continue to be exploited, maltreated, enslaved, prey to violence and illicit trafficking. Still too many children live in exile, as refugees, at times lost at sea, particularly in the waters of the Mediterranean. Today, in acknowledging this, we feel shame before God, before God who became a child....

In a world which daily discards tons of food and medicine there are children, hungry and suffering from easily curable diseases, who cry out in vain. In an age which insists on the protection of minors, there is a flourishing trade in weapons which end up in the hands of child-soldiers; there is a ready market for goods produced by the slave labor of small children. Their cry is stifled: the cry of these children is stifled! They must fight, they must work, they cannot cry! But their mothers cry for them, as modern-day Rachels: they weep for their children, and they refuse to be consoled (cf. Mt 2:18).

HOMILY, MANGER SQUARE, BETHLEHEM
SUNDAY, MAY 25, 2014

MARY, MOTHER OF EVERY WOUNDED FAMILY

There are families here today which suffered greatly in the long conflict which tore open the heart of Sri Lanka.... But Our Lady remains with you always. She is the mother of every home, of every wounded family, of all who are seeking to return to a peaceful existence. Today we thank her for protecting the people of Sri Lanka from so many dangers, past and present. Mary never forgot her children on this resplendent island. Just as she never left the side of her Son on the Cross, so she never left the side of her suffering Sri Lankan children.

MARIAN PRAYER,
SHRINE OF OUR LADY OF THE ROSARY,
MADHU, SRI LANKA
WEDNESDAY, JANUARY 14, 2015

Pope Francis @Pontifex · January 1, 2015

"How many innocent people and children suffer in the world! Lord, grant us your peace!"

THE CHURCH IS HOME TO ALL

We must ask ourselves: are we up to the task of bringing Christ into this area, or better still, of bringing others to meet Christ? Can we walk alongside the pilgrim of today's world as Jesus walked with those companions to Emmaus, warming their hearts on the way and bringing them to an encounter with the Lord? Are we able to communicate the face of a Church which is "home" to all? We sometimes speak of a Church that has its doors closed, but here we are contemplating much more than a Church with open doors, much more! We must, together, build this "home," build this Church, make this "home." A Church with closed doors or open doors; the task is to move forward and help build the Church. The challenge is to rediscover, through the means of social communication as well as by personal contact, the beauty that is at the heart of our existence and journey, the beauty of faith and of the beauty of the encounter with Christ.... This is the path. This is the challenge.

ADDRESS TO THE PONTIFICAL COUNCIL FOR SOCIAL
COMMUNICATIONS, THE VATICAN
SATURDAY, SEPTEMBER 21, 2013

LORD, HEAR OUR PRAYER!

Evening falls on our assembly. It is the hour at which one willingly returns home to meet at the same table, in the depth of affection, of the good that has been done and received, of the encounters which warm the heart and make it grow, good wine which hastens the unending feast in the days of man.

It is also the weightiest hour for one who finds himself face to face with his own loneliness, in the bitter twilight of shattered dreams and broken plans; how many people trudge through the day in the blind alley of resignation, of abandonment, even resentment: in how many homes the wine of joy has been less plentiful, and therefore, also the zest—the very wisdom—for life. Let us make our prayer heard for one another this evening, a prayer for all....

Our listening and our discussion on the family, loved with the gaze of Christ, will become a providential occasion with which to renew—according to the example of St. Francis—the Church and society.

ADDRESS DURING THE MEETING ON THE FAMILY,
ST. PETER'S SQUARE
SATURDAY, OCTOBER 4, 2014

GO FORWARD WITH PATIENCE AND TRUST

The family is a community which provides help, which celebrates life and is fruitful. Once we realize this, we will once more be able to see how the family continues to be a rich human resource, as opposed to a problem or an institution in crisis....

Families at their best actively communicate by their witness the beauty and the richness of the relationship between man and woman, and between parents and children. We are not fighting to defend the past. Rather, with patience and trust, we are working to build a better future for the world in which we live.

MESSAGE FOR 49TH WORLD COMMUNICATIONS DAY,
FROM THE VATICAN
FRIDAY, JANUARY 23, 2015

CHAPTER FIVE

~ The Role and Responsibility of Elders ~

"Where there is no honor for elders, there is no future for the young."

—POPE FRANCIS, MARCH 4, 2015

My Grandmother's Lessons of Faith

I had the great blessing of growing up in a family in which faith was lived in a simple, practical way. However it was my paternal grandmother in particular who influenced my journey of faith. She was a woman who talked to us about Jesus, who taught us the catechism. I always remember that on the evening of Good Friday she would take us to the candle-light procession, and at the end of this procession "the dead Christ" would arrive. Our grandmother would make us children kneel down, and she would say to us: "Look, he is dead, but tomorrow he will rise!" This was how I received my first Christian proclamation, from this very woman, from my grandmother! This is really beautiful! The first proclamation at home, in the family! And this makes me think of the love of so many mothers and grandmothers in the transmission of faith.

ADDRESS TO MEMBERS OF ECCLESIAL MOVEMENTS,
ST. PETER'S SQUARE
SATURDAY, MAY 18, 2013

Pope Francis @Pontifex · May 8, 2014

In our families we learn to love and to recognize the dignity of all, especially of the elderly.

The Lord Never Discards Us

In today's catechesis we continue our reflection on grandparents, considering the value and importance of their role in the family. I do so by placing myself in their shoes, because I too belong to this age group. When I was in the Philippines, the Filipino people greeted me saying "Lolo Kiko"—meaning Grandpa Francis....

It is true that society tends to discard us, but the Lord definitely does not! The Lord never discards us. He calls us to follow him in every age of life, and old age has a grace and a mission too, a true vocation from the Lord. Old age is a vocation. It is not yet time to "pull in the oars." This period of life is different from those before, there is no doubt; we even have to somewhat "invent it ourselves," because our societies are not ready, spiritually and morally, to appreciate the true value of this stage of life....

Christian spirituality has also been caught somewhat by surprise, with regard to outlining a kind of spirituality of the elderly. But thanks be to God there is no shortage of the testimony of elderly saints, both men and women!

GENERAL AUDIENCE, ST. PETER'S SQUARE
WEDNESDAY, MARCH 11, 2015

The Testimony of the Elderly

I was really moved by the "Day dedicated to the elderly" that we had here in St. Peter's Square last year, the Square was full. I listened to the stories of elderly people who devote themselves to others, and to stories of married couples, who said: "We are celebrating our 50th wedding anniversary, we are celebrating our 60th wedding anniversary." It is important to present this to young people who tire so easily; the testimony of the elderly in fidelity is important. There were so many in this Square that day. It is a reflection to continue, in both the ecclesial and civil spheres.

GENERAL AUDIENCE, ST. PETER'S SQUARE
WEDNESDAY, MARCH 11, 2015

The Insurance of Our Faith

To the elderly:

I was saying to Salvatore that perhaps there are people missing here, perhaps the most important of all: grandparents! The elderly are not here, yet they are the "insurance" of our faith, the "old folks."... The elderly! They are our wisdom, they are the wisdom of the Church—the elderly whom we so often discard, grandparents, the elderly.... Grandmothers and grandfathers are our strength and our wisdom. May the Lord always give us wise elders! Elderly men and women who can pass on to us the memory of our people, the memory of the Church. May they also give us what the Letter to the Hebrews says about them: a sense of joy. It says that our forebears, our elders, greeted God's promises from afar. May this be what they teach us.

ADDRESS TO PARTICIPANTS IN THE
37TH NATIONAL CONVOCATION
OF THE RENEWAL IN THE HOLY SPIRIT,
OLYMPIC STADIUM, ROME
SUNDAY, JUNE 1, 2014

A Wealth Not to Be Ignored

While we are young, we are led to ignore old age, as if it were a disease to keep away from; then when we become old, especially if we are poor, if we are sick and alone, we experience the shortcomings of a society programmed for efficiency, which consequently ignores its elderly. And the elderly are a wealth not to be ignored.

Benedict XVI, visiting a home for the elderly, used clear and prophetic words, saying in this way: "The quality of a society, I mean of a civilization, is also judged by how it treats elderly people and by the place it gives them in community life" (November 12, 2012). It's true, attention to the elderly makes the difference in a civilization. Is there attention to the elderly in a civilization? Is there room for the elderly? This civilization will move forward if it knows how to respect wisdom, the wisdom of the elderly. In a civilization in which there is no room for the elderly or where they are thrown away because they create problems, this society carries with it the virus of death.

GENERAL AUDIENCE, ST. PETER'S SQUARE
WEDNESDAY, MARCH 4, 2015

An Enduring Chorus of Praise

The prayer of the elderly is a beautiful thing. We are able to thank the Lord for the benefits received, and fill the emptiness of ingratitude that surrounds us. We are able to intercede for the expectations of younger generations and give dignity to the memory and sacrifices of past generations. We are able to remind ambitious young people that a life without love is a barren life. We are able say to young people who are afraid that anxiety about the future can be overcome. We are able to teach the young who are overly self-absorbed that there is more joy in giving than in receiving. Grandfathers and grandmothers form the enduring "chorus" of a great spiritual sanctuary, where prayers of supplication and songs of praise sustain the community which toils and struggles in the field of life.

GENERAL AUDIENCE, ST. PETER'S SQUARE
WEDNESDAY, MARCH 11, 2015

CARRIERS OF MEMORY AND WISDOM

The elderly have always been and still are protagonists in the Church. Today more than ever the Church must set an example for the whole of society that, despite their inevitable and sometimes grave "ailments," the elderly are always important; indeed, they are indispensable. They carry the memory and wisdom of life to hand down to others, and they participate fully in the Church's mission. Let us remember that, in God's eyes, human life always retains its value far beyond any discriminating vision.

ADDRESS TO PARTICIPANTS IN THE 28TH
INTERNATIONAL CONFERENCE FOR HEALTH CARE
WORKERS, PAUL VI AUDIENCE HALL
SATURDAY, NOVEMBER 23, 2013

Pope Francis @Pontifex · February 27, 2014

In a family it is normal to take charge of those who need help. Do not be afraid of frailty!

LET US BECOME POETS OF PRAYER

The Gospel comes to meet us with a really moving and encouraging image. It is the image of Simeon and Anna, who are spoken of in the Gospel of Jesus' childhood, composed by St. Luke. They were certainly elderly, the "old man," Simeon, and the "prophetess," Anna, who was 84 years old. This woman did not hide her age. The Gospel says that they awaited the coming of God every day, with great trust, for many years. They truly wanted to see Him that day, to grasp the signs, to understand the origin. By then, they were also perhaps more resigned to die first. That long wait, however, continued to occupy their whole life, having no commitments more important than this: to await the Lord and pray. So, when Mary and Joseph went to the temple to fulfill the provisions of the Law, Simeon and Anna moved quickly, inspired by the Holy Spirit (cf. Lk 2:27). The burden of age and waiting disappeared in an instant. They recognized the Child, and discovered new strength, for a new task: to give thanks for and bear witness to this Sign from God. Simeon improvised a beautiful hymn of jubilation (cf. Lk 2:29-32)—in that moment he was a poet—and Anna became the first woman to preach of Jesus: she "spoke of him to all who were looking for the redemption of Jerusalem" (Lk 2:38).

Dear grandparents, dear elderly, let us follow in the footsteps of these extraordinary elders! Let us too become like poets of prayer: let us develop a taste for finding our own words, let us once again grasp those which teach us the Word of God.

GENERAL AUDIENCE, ST. PETER'S SQUARE
WEDNESDAY, MARCH 11, 2015

THE TREASURE OF A COMMUNITY

The care given to the elderly, like that of children, is an indicator of the quality of a community. When the elderly are tossed aside, when the elderly are isolated and sometimes fade away due to a lack of care, it's an awful sign! How nice instead is that alliance between young and old that I see here, where everyone gives and receives! The elderly and their prayers are a treasure for Sant'Egidio. A people who don't protect their elderly, who don't take care of their young, is a people without a future, a people without hope. Because the young—the children, the youth—and the old carry history forward. The children, the young, rightly have their biological strength; and the elderly offer their memory. But when a community loses its memory, it's over…it's over. It's awful to see a community, a people, a culture, that's lost its memory.

ADDRESS TO THE SANT'EGIDIO COMMUNITY,
BASILICA OF "SANTA MARIA IN TRASTEVERE"
SUNDAY, JUNE 15, 2014

The Discourse of the Aged

In the tradition of the Church there is a wealth of wisdom that has always supported a culture of closeness to the elderly, a disposition of warm and supportive companionship in this final phase of life. This tradition is rooted in Sacred Scripture, as these passages from the Book of Sirach attest: "Do not disregard the discourse of the aged, for they themselves learned from their fathers; because from them you will gain understanding and learn how to give an answer in time of need" (Sir 8:9).

The Church cannot and does not want to conform to a mentality of impatience, and much less of indifference and contempt, towards old age. We must reawaken the collective sense of gratitude, of appreciation, of hospitality, which makes the elder feel like a living part of his community.

GENERAL AUDIENCE, ST. PETER'S SQUARE
WEDNESDAY, MARCH 4, 2015

SHOW RESPECT FOR THE ELDERLY

Saint Paul urges Timothy, who was a pastor and hence a father to the community, to show respect for the elderly and members of families. He tells him to do so like a son: treating "older men as fathers," "older women as mothers" and "younger women as sisters" (cf. 1 Tim 5:1).... Like the Virgin Mary, who, though she became the mother of the Messiah, felt herself driven by the love of God taking flesh within her to hasten to her elderly relative....

We can imagine that the Virgin Mary, visiting the home of Elizabeth, would have heard her and her husband Zechariah praying in the words of today's responsorial psalm: "You, O Lord, are my hope, my trust, O Lord, from my youth.... Do not cast me off in the time of old age, do not forsake me when my strength is spent.... Even to old age and grey hairs, O God, do not forsake me, until I proclaim your might to all the generations to come" (Ps 71:5, 9, 18). The young Mary listened, and she kept all these things in her heart. The wisdom of Elizabeth and Zechariah enriched her young spirit.

HOMILY, MASS FOR THE ELDERLY, ST. PETER'S SQUARE
SUNDAY, SEPTEMBER 28, 2014

A Most Precious Heritage

Grandparents, who have received the blessing to see their children's children (cf. Ps 128:6), are entrusted with a great responsibility: to transmit their life experience, their family history, the history of a community, of a people; to share wisdom with simplicity, and the faith itself—the most precious heritage! Happy is the family who has grandparents close by! A grandfather is a father twice over and a grandmother is a mother twice over. In those countries where religious persecution has been cruel—I am thinking, for instance, of Albania, where I was last Sunday—in those countries it was the grandparents who brought the children to be baptized in secret, to give them the faith. Well done! They were brave in persecution and they saved the faith in those countries!

ADDRESS OF POPE FRANCIS TO THE ELDERLY,
ST. PETER'S SQUARE
SUNDAY, SEPTEMBER 28, 2014

ELDERS ARE NOT ALIENS

Our elders are men and women, fathers and mothers, who came before us on our own road, in our own house, in our daily battle for a worthy life. They are men and women from whom we have received so much. The elder is not an alien. We are that elder: in the near or far future, but inevitably, even if we don't think it. And if we don't learn how to treat the elder better, that is how we will be treated.

GENERAL AUDIENCE, ST. PETER'S SQUARE
WEDNESDAY, MARCH 4, 2015

Pope Francis @Pontifex · May 6, 2014

A society which abandons children and the elderly severs its roots and darkens its future.

We Must Fight for Our Values

Look, at this moment I think our world civilization has gone beyond its limits. It has gone beyond its limits because it has made money into such a god that we are now faced with a philosophy and a practice which exclude the two ends of life that are most full of promise for people. They exclude the elderly, obviously. You could easily think there is a kind of hidden euthanasia, that is, we don't take care of the elderly; but there is also a cultural euthanasia, because we don't allow them to speak, we don't allow them to act. And there is the exclusion of the young. The percentage of our young people without work, without employment, is very high, and we have a generation with no experience of the dignity gained through work. This civilization, in other words, has led us to exclude the two peaks that make up our future. As for the young, they must emerge, they must assert themselves. The young must go out to fight for values, to fight for these values; and the elderly must open their mouths, the elderly must open their mouths and teach us! Pass on to us the wisdom of the peoples!

ADDRESS TO THE YOUTH OF ARGENTINA,
28TH WORLD YOUTH DAY, RIO DE JANEIRO
THURSDAY, JULY 25, 2013

THE MISSION OF THE ELDERLY

Prayer unceasingly purifies the heart. Praise and supplication to God prevents the heart from becoming hardened by resentment and selfishness. How awful is the cynicism of an elderly person who has lost the meaning of his testimony, who scorns the young and does not communicate the wisdom of life! How beautiful, however, is the encouragement an elderly person manages to pass on to a young person who is seeking the meaning of faith and of life! It is truly the mission of grandparents, the vocation of the elderly. The words of grandparents have special value for the young. And the young know it. I still carry with me, always, in my breviary, the words my grandmother consigned to me in writing on the day of my priestly ordination. I read them often and they do me good.

GENERAL AUDIENCE, ST. PETER'S SQUARE
WEDNESDAY, MARCH 11, 2015

LED BY THE HOLY SPIRIT

The Church that cares for children and the elderly becomes the mother of generations of believers and, at the same time, serves human society because a spirit of love, familiarity and solidarity helps all people to rediscover the fatherhood and motherhood of God.

And when I read this Gospel passage (Lk. 2:22–29), I like to think about the fact that those young people, Joseph and Mary, as well as the Child, abide by the Law. Four times St. Luke says: in fulfillment of the Law. They are obedient to the Law, the young people! And the two elders, they are the ones to make noise! Simeon at that moment invents his own liturgy and praises, he praises God. And the old woman goes and talks, she preaches through her chatter: "Look at him!" They are so free! And three times it states that the elders are led by the Holy Spirit. The young by the law, the elders by the Holy Spirit. Look to our elderly people who have this spirit within them, listen to them!

ADDRESS TO PARTICIPANTS IN THE PLENARY ASSEMBLY
OF THE PONTIFICAL COUNCIL FOR THE FAMILY,
CLEMENTINE HALL
FRIDAY, OCTOBER 25, 2013

VISIT YOUR ELDERS!

I remember, when I was visiting a retirement home, I spoke with each person and I frequently heard this:

"How are you? And your children?"

"Well, well."

"How many do you have?"

"Many."

"And do they come to visit you?"

"Oh sure, yes, always, yes, they come."

"When was the last time they came?"

I remember an elderly woman who said to me: "Mmm, for Christmas." It was August! Eight months without being visited by her children, abandoned for eight months! This is called mortal sin, understand?

GENERAL AUDIENCE, ST. PETER'S SQUARE
WEDNESDAY, MARCH 4, 2015

HOMES FOR THE ELDERLY

Not every older person, grandfather, or grandmother, has a family who can take in him or her. And so homes for the elderly are welcome...but may they be real homes and not prisons! And may they truly be for the good of the elderly, and not for the interests of anyone else! They must not be institutions where the elderly live forgotten, hidden and neglected. I feel close to the many elderly who live in these institutions, and I think with gratitude of those who go to visit them and care for them. Homes for the elderly should be the "lungs" of humanity in a town, a neighborhood, or a parish. They should be the "sanctuaries" of humanity where one who is old and weak is cared for and protected like a big brother or sister. It is so good to go visit an elderly person!

ADDRESS TO THE ELDERLY,
ST. PETER'S SQUARE SUNDAY,
SEPTEMBER 28, 2014

Pope Francis @Pontifex · August 17, 2013
We cannot sleep peacefully while babies are dying of hunger and the elderly are without medical assistance.